The Have It All Woman

Take your life from overwhelmed
to empowered

SUSAN SLY

The Have It All Woman
Written by Susan Sly

Published by Sound Concepts

www.susanslybooks.com

ISBN 978-0-9737317-3-6
Library and Archives Canada Cataloguing in Publication

Sly, Susan, 1972-
The Have It All Woman : a practical guide to achieving balance, abundance and the life of your dreams / Susan Sly.

Includes
ISBN 978-0-9737317-3-6

1. Women--Conduct of life. 2. Self-realization in women.
I. Title.

HQ1221.S59 2008 158.1082 C2007-906821-9

Manufactured and Printed in The USA

DEDICATION & ACKNOWLEDGEMENTS

"Everything we do should be a result of our gratitude for what God has done for us."

— Lauryn Hill, *Singer*

I gratefully dedicate this book to God, my family and *Have It All Women* everywhere. Chris you are my rock, my angel and the ever-present reminder that dreams do come true. Avery, AJ, Sarai and Emery—thank you for blessing my life. I am honored to be your mother. Thank you also to my Dad for Sunday afternoon football, quests for giant pumpkins and teaching me that whatever I wanted was possible. Thank you to my mother for giving me the gift of faith.

This book is also dedicated to my late grandmothers Agnes and Lois. You were, and continue to be, forces to be reckoned with. Thank you to my aunts Gloria, Valerie, Alice, Ruth, Mae, Dianne, Pauline and Verna. You taught me how to be focused, dedicated and do it all with style.

Thank you to the many wonderful people who inspired me to write this book. Thank you to Dr. Tony O'Donnell for his many encouraging words. Thank you to Jack Canfield and Dr. John Gray for endorsing the book and my publisher, Sound Concepts, for embracing every new idea I have.

A very special thank you to Diana Frerick for her stunning cover design.

Thank you especially for our amazing Step Into Your Power™ team: Tisha, Sandy, P.K. and Christina. I feel so honored to collaborate with you.

Lastly, this book is dedicated to fabulous women everywhere—may we inspire one another always.

Great Complementary Reading

Health

Skinny Bitch, by Rory Freedman and Kim Barnouin

Miracle Super Foods That Heal, by Dr. Tony O'Donnell

Prescription for Nutritional Healing, by Phyllis Balch

Relationships

The 5 Love Languages, by Gary Chapman

Radical Forgiveness, by Colin Tipping

Men are From Mars, Women are from Venus,
by Dr. John Gray

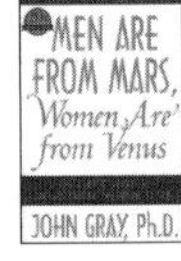

Self-Worth

In the Meantime, by Iyanla Vanzant

Excuses Be Gone, by Dr. Wayne Dyer

Excuse Me, Your Life is Waiting, by Lynn Grabhorn

Money and Prosperity

Rich Dad, Poor Dad, by Robert Kiosaki

The Richest Man in Babylon, by George C. Clasen

The Power of Focus,
by Les Hewitt, Jack Canfield and Mark Victor Hansen

The Success Principles, by Jack Canfield

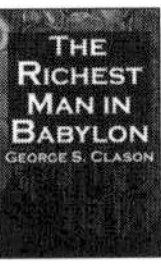

Connect With Susan

On Facebook at www.facebook.com/susanslylive

On Twitter at susan_sly

On the WEB at www.susansly.com

Receive the Best Experience from this Book

This book is written with love and the words contained within each and every chapter are intended to help you live a more blissful, joy-filled, abundant and prosperous life. You are Divinely created and yes, you can *have it all.*

This book is divided into three specific life areas—health, relationships and money. Within these areas are sub-categories—faith and spirituality, self-love, primary and secondary relationships, assets versus liabilities and the overriding principles of joy and fun. These concepts are sub-divided within the *have it all woman's* life pyramid.

There are specific exercises to complete at the end every chapter of this book. To receive the greatest results, I encourage you to stop and do every individual exercise. Many women feel completely overwhelmed in one or more aspects of their lives and it is easy to gloss over something, including those things that might prove highly effective. When you come to an exercise, stop, breathe, and take time to complete it from start to finish.

In addition to using the "Four D" principle which is explained in Chapter One, there is a powerful affirmation at the end of each chapter. This will assist you in absorbing the work you have done. Stop, take a deep breath, and recite the affirmation at least three to four times. You may also wish to write the affirmation out and place it on your bedside table.

Many readers have contacted us to share the wonderful progress that has occurred by reading this book. Men have even written to me sharing how this book has helped enhance communication in relationships and even assist them in greater understanding of the important women in their lives. Take time to savor this book like a fine wine and let the aroma of these words fill your soul. In doing this you will be well on your way to becoming a true *have it all woman.*

Please note the some names have been changed to protect identity.

With Love and Appreciation,

Life is an opportunity, benefit from it.
Life is beauty, admire it.
Life is a dream, realize it.
Life is a challenge, meet it.
Life is a duty, complete it.
Life is a game, play it.
Life is a promise, fulfill it.
Life is sorrow, overcome it.
Life is a song, sing it.
Life is a struggle, accept it.
Life is a tragedy, confront it.
Life is an adventure, dare it.
Life is luck, make it.
Life is too precious, do not destroy it.
Life is life, fight for it.

— Mother Teresa

TABLE OF CONTENTS

Foreword i

Chapter One
Step One—Simply Decide 1

Chapter Two
Step Two—Creating a Clearing in Your Life 29

Chapter Three
Step Three—Creating Abundant Health..53

Chapter Four
Step Four—Faith...99

Chapter Five
Step Five—Self-love 113

Chapter Six
Step Six—Fulfilling Relationships 127

Chapter Seven
Step Seven—Creating Financial Ease..171

Chapter Eight
Step Eight—Giving Back 209

Chapter Nine
Step Nine—Girls Just Want to Have Fun 219

Conclusion...229

Personal Endorsements...231

"Women are like teabags.
We don't know our true strength
until we are in hot water!"

— Eleanor Roosevelt, *First Lady*

FOREWORD

by Andrea Frank Henkart

In this age of technology and telecommuting, fast food and the fast lane, balancing work and family remain a major challenge. Is it any wonder that women everywhere ask, "Where's the instruction manual?!"

As we try to find balance, our own needs and desires often fall by the wayside. If we ignore our health and well-being, we may lose our ability to efficiently cope with the everyday ups and downs. On the other hand, if we focus on our own dreams, goals, desires and needs, or if we dare put ourselves first, we are often considered selfish. This can lead to misunderstandings, overwhelm and a rapid breakdown in communication with family, friends and colleagues.

As a wife and the mother of two beautiful, grown children and the author of seven books on childbirth, health and wellness for the family, and communication skills for parents and kids, I know what overwhelm looks like firsthand. I am an entrepreneur; I own two businesses and run an extremely successful network marketing business. As an international inspirational speaker, I have worked with over 11,000 teens and their parents around the globe. I do my best to practice what I preach, but it has not always been easy.

Along the way, I discovered that when life gets stressful, I always have a choice. I can choose to empower myself and transform my own reality by changing my actions and my thoughts. By focusing on the good things in life, I can literally switch a negative attitude to a positive one. This one particular action creates an opportunity to change how I approach each day. It becomes even easier when I live every day with awareness, appreciation and gratitude.

So, how do we find creative ways to feed our souls and nurture our own bodies? To paraphrase my friend and fellow author, Susan Sly, once you decide who you are and what you want, and are prepared to put in the effort to get there, the possibilities become endless. If you choose to succeed, if you want to make a positive and significant impact on others, if you want to be extraordinary, then this book is for you. It will change your life in ways you never dreamed possible. It certainly changed mine.

Susan wants every woman to know that we are "in process" and that whatever we desire to have or be is "out there" waiting for us to claim. In this book, she provides us with seven inspiring chapters filled with anecdotes, principles and exercises that help guide us toward our desired goals. Susan is dedicated to helping women define and identify their raison d'etre. It is indeed a journey that begins with identifying who we are, then prioritizing our lives, including our health, and making ourselves available to receive all that is available to us.

Susan has a story to tell. It is a story about her, and a story about you and me. It is a story written by one woman for all women who are willing to invest the time and effort to learn, grow, and empower themselves in the process. In this book, as in life, Susan is candid, vulnerable, uplifting and encouraging. Writing from her own experience of challenge and triumph, she challenges her readers to go for their dreams. She wants women to know they can *have it all*; that they can - in their own way and while maintaining their own identity – be true *Have It All Women*.

I had the joyous pleasure of spending time with Susan and her beautiful family. Her commitment to her children, her husband, her friends, and her own self is truly inspiring. Because of who she is and how she lives her life, her wisdom, strength, compassion and vulnerability have inspired me. Therefore, it is with great joy that I invite you, the reader, to step into your power, make an impact on your world and become what you were destined to be – a *Have It All Woman*.

Andrea Frank Henkart
Marin County, CA
www.coolcommunication.com

Andrea is a bestselling author who has appeared on Oprah and many other syndicated television programs.

CHAPTER ONE

Step 1: Simply Decide

"From now on I am going to own myself and be true to myself. I no longer want to live someone else's idea of what and who I should be. I am going to be me!"

— Diana, *Princess of Wales*

CHAPTER ONE

Step 1: Simply Decide

The 18-Inch Journey That Lasts a Lifetime

"If you gave someone your heart and they died, did they take it with them? Did you spend the rest of forever with a hole inside you that couldn't be filled?"

— Jodi Picoult, *Nineteen Minutes*

Take a moment and consider the very distance from your head to your heart. Relatively, and anatomically speaking, it is only about eighteen inches. That may not truly seem very much; something that could indeed be travelled in a nanosecond. The reality is, for most people, that this journey is one that lasts an entire lifetime.

Our brain, one hundred million cells within a body of one hundred trillion cells; it is the epicenter of thought. Our heart, smaller than the brain and yet also extremely important in that one can be brain dead and survive on life support and yet once the heart ceases to beat, we are at the mercy of death. Science has not truly discovered the power of the heart, though we know that somehow there is much more to human "beingness" than simply thinking; somehow our heart is quintessential to our survival.

Consider, if you will, the notion that trusting our heart may indeed be the secret to unlocking a life so rich we can barely imagine it. Ponder the notion that our busy minds, approximately 60,000 thoughts per day, of which over eighty percent are negative, are actually usurping our ability to have a life that is fulfilling, balanced and whole. What if, a seemingly short eighteen-inch journey was all that it took to creating more in your life than you ever imagined? Perhaps it is.

Although a physically short distance, these eighteen inches are actually some of the most treacherous terrain we can ever face. As we follow our heart, learn to trust in ourselves and release the wielding power of our overactive minds we can second-guess our progress often self-sabotaging and reverting back to old behaviors. To truly live a *have it all* life will mean following your heart, taking this journey and perhaps stepping into a deeper level of trust and faith that you have ever allowed yourself to surrender to before.

The Ugly Duckling

"Let me see the egg which will not burst," said the old visitor. "You may be sure it is a turkey's egg. I was once cheated in that way, and had much anxiety and trouble with the young ones, for they are afraid of the water. Must I say it to you, I could not get them to venture in. I quacked and I clacked, but it was no use. Let me see the egg. Yes, that`s a turkey's egg. Let it lie there, and teach the other children to swim."

"I think I will sit on it a little longer," said the Duck. "I've sat so long now that I can sit a few days more."

"Just as you please," said the old Duck; and she went away.

At last the great egg burst. "Piep! piep!" said the little one, and crept forth. It was very large and very ugly. The Duck looked at it.

"It,s a very large duckling," said she; "none of the others look like that: can it really be a turkey chick? Well, we shall soon find out. It must go into the water, even if I have to thrust it in myself."

— Excerpted from Hans Christian Andersen's *The Ugly Duckling*

Growing up I was that gawky girl who no one liked. I was fat, had bucked teeth, and had dark skin in a town where hardly anyone else did. My parents were divorced in a time that no one's parents were and I was consistently dressed in clothes from the second-hand store. In other words, I wasn’t that girl that would have won the local beauty pageant, was not invited for play dates and was always picked last for any kind of team.

When I lived with my mother we were very poor. For religious reasons, she wouldn't allow me to wear jeans like the other girls and all of my bargain shop dresses were the brunt of constant jokes at school. I was bullied and physically tormented. School and the play yard were very scary places. I longed to fit in.

When I went to live with my Dad I felt inept, even in my own family. My cousins were lean and gorgeous. My aunts were sleek and beautiful. I was the odd one. Many times I overheard conversations where someone in my family would be discussing my “weight problem.” I would cry knowing that I wasn't good enough for my own family.

I remember once, at the age of ten, punching myself in the stomach repeatedly and yelling at the girl in the mirror, “I hate you,” over and over again. The fat didn't go away, and the red fist marks remained. It felt good to inflict pain, so this became my ritual, standing in front of the mirror and punching myself twenty-five times every day. I hated me.

In the day time I was bullied at school. I was called the “N” word and “chinky, chinky China man.” There were other names as well, “loser,” “bubba,” and “fat-so.” Many nights I lay awake praying to die; I couldn’t understand why God was punishing me by making me this way. I do not know if my dad or my grandmother knew how much emotional pain I was in. In our family, we did not talk about our feelings; we swallowed our emotions and we soldiered on.

Growing up, my favorite book was The Ugly Duckling. I knew exactly how that duckling felt. My fat hung out of my skating and gymnastics suits. People mocked me. I was never good enough. Just like the ugly duckling, I wanted to go away from the world that reminded me on a daily basis of all that I was not. At night I prayed to God that someday I would become a swan.

My transformation didn't happen magically like it does in fairy tales. There was no Fairy Godmother to wave a magic wand. It took decades to get comfortable in my own skin –to journey from my head to my heart. It took faith, surrender, trust, dedication and determination. I had to be willing to do what others would not, including making decisions that were seemingly against the norm.

You may be feeling overwhelmed, stressed out, insignificant, depressed, hopeless or inadequate and the intention of this book is to be your version of a fairy godmother with the purpose to inspire you to take control of your life and put you on the journey to having it all.

Throughout this book are the lessons that have been garnered on the journey to having it all – a journey which continues on to this day. Sometimes I still see the gawky, overweight girl in the mirror. I embrace her because through her eyes I take nothing for granted. In reading this book and going through the exercises, I pray that you find the answers you seek for your own personal transformation.

On the media tour to promote the initial release of the draft copy of this book, I was asked repeatedly if women can truly *have it all.* My answer was always yes, the reason being that, as women, although we may appear to want different things; ultimately having it all comes down to three areas – health, relationships and money.

When the book was first released I was doing a promotional event with Mark Victor Hansen, co-author of the New York Times bestselling book series, Chicken Soup for the Soul™. A girl with black hair, black fingernails, dark eye make-up and multiple piercings came up to the table to buy a copy of the *Have It All Woman*. She didn't speak; she simply purchased the book and walked away. The next morning a fresh faced, smiling girl approached the table. She said, "You probably don't remember me," and truthfully I didn't at first but on further inspection found her to be the Goth-looking girl from the previous evening.

She said, "I stayed up and read your book all night. I had been planning to kill myself and now I intend to live." We both welled up with tears and in that moment I realized that the time spent writing this book was absolutely worth it. One young girl had decided to live.

Today the *Have It All Woman* is in libraries all over North America. It has been read by a wide range of women, from those in shelters to book clubs in cities and towns – all seeking the answers to creating more in their lives. The objective is to help women realize that all things are possible; anyone can transform.

Sometimes it feels overwhelming to even think about where we can be versus where we are in our lives right now. You may also feel like the Ugly Duckling; however, I know you are a beautiful swan.

I have been working with women for years and if I could wave a magic wand to help you get to the next level in your life, I would. The journey to having it all is going to be fraught with choices, some easy and some hard. The truth is that the journey to having it all is where the true success lies; it is the woman we become in the process.

I wish you every joy and happiness on your own personal quest for betterment in all areas of your life. You are already on the path to becoming a *Have It All Woman*.

Who Are You Really?

"I live for the present always. I accept this risk. I don't deny the past, but it's a page to turn."

—Juliette Binoche, *Actress*

In the year 2000, soon after I was diagnosed with multiple sclerosis, and before I spiraled into financial ruin, a friend and I were on the phone and out of the blue he asked me one of the most important questions of my life. He said, "Susan, you define yourself by what you do and what you own; however, if you lost everything tomorrow and were all alone in the world with no money, no job, no family, no friends, no home or anything at all – who would you be?"

I was stunned; he was so right. Like many women, I defined myself by my roles as opposed to defining myself as an individual. There are many thought-provoking, life-altering questions out there, such as "Will you marry me?" And "Did the stick turn blue or pink?" This was, and remains, one of the most life-altering questions I have ever faced. In my seminars and courses I use this question to help women to step into their personal power. When we know who we are, life gets a lot clearer.

Having the certainty of our definition of self assists us with every imaginable decision, from the seemingly mundane to the life-altering.

At the time I didn't have an answer for my friend. But he was right. According to me and the rest of my world, I was a gym owner, personal trainer, fitness instructor, mother, wife and media personality. But really, who was I? I didn't know.

I went out on my bike the next day. It was windy and cold, a brutal February day in Canada. I rode and rode for hours with one question on my mind. Who am I?

The answer did come. It came to me in the form of a word while I was in prayer. The word that came was "teacher." There was something I was meant to teach.

When my world collapsed, the word "teacher" stayed with me. It gave me solitude in knowing that surely I must have lost my health, my marriage, and everything else for a purpose. There was something I was supposed to learn so I could teach it. In the darkest moments it gave me peace.

I have revisited this exercise and have now come to realize that, like you and everyone else on Earth, I am love, I am a child of God and I am infinite potential.

I encourage you to take a moment, right now, and meditate on the question—who am I? Initially your roles may come to mind; mother, wife, your job, and the descriptions of what you do and not who you truly are. Go beyond these roles, travel beyond the realm of your ego and allow for the answer to come. It may not come right away; however, one day, perhaps when you least expect it, it will. In that moment you will know that you, too, are love.

The Curve in the Road

"Turn your words into wisdom." — Oprah Winfrey, *Media Personality*

In almost every woman's life comes at least one tipping point—a time when things could go either way. Our health, our relationships, our finances, or all of the aforementioned combined are hanging in the balance. We question ourselves; we weigh the outcome of our decisions. Sometimes we wonder if we can truly go on. These are the moments that either refine or define us; these are the times when our resolve is tested and our hopes and dreams are put on the backburner as we struggle to find the answers.

The year 2003 was one of those refining moments for me. The previous three years had been some of the toughest of my life. I had been struggling with multiple sclerosis for three years, faced financial ruin and was definitely not the mother or partner I wanted to be. After years of trying to be everything for everyone and essentially doing it all, I felt that I had hit rock bottom.

At night I would toss and turn in physical agony. I felt as though I wanted to tear the skin off my body. The pain was intense. I would get up after a sleepless night, feeling like I had been run over by a truck, drink several cups of coffee, give my partner, Chris, a peck on the cheek, get my one and six year old ready for a trip to Grandma's and school respectively, and head to my job at a non-profit where I would put on my "game face" hiding my illness despite occasionally slurring my speech and downing Advil throughout the day.

Most days, if I didn't have meeting, I would sneak home for lunch and just lie on the sofa. Sometimes I would cry; being at home alone provided me with the safety to release my feelings of frustration. I thought about suicide a lot. My body was shutting down and there didn't seem like there was much I could do about it.

The MS diagnosis had come in January of 2000. Despite the shock, I was not overly surprised because intuitively I knew that something was wrong. I had been exhausted, started dropping things, sometimes had difficulty enunciating words and experienced a great degree of numbness and tingling. Initially my doctor had said it was just stress, though I knew there was more to it.

Because of my highly physical lifestyle, as an athlete, personal trainer, fitness instructor and gym owner, it would have been easy to simply think that my body was just under a lot of stress and that I needed to slow down. However, slowing down was not in my nature and I pushed myself harder. I pushed myself past the fatigue; I soldiered through the increasing agony of my body fighting back.

After the diagnosis there were many doctors who all had different opinions on what to do. My adrenals had also shut down, which led to my thyroid underperforming. I had my general practitioner, an endocrinologist and of course was referred to a neurologist. I also chose to see a chiropractor and a naturopath.

Not long after my diagnosis other aspects of my life began to unravel. My marriage fell apart. We lost our business. I was humiliated. For a period of time I questioned God. How could this happen to me? What had I done to deserve this? I was angry. I cried until it felt that there was no more left and my stomach ached from wrenching my body with sobs. I felt incredibly alone though I had felt lonely within my marriage for a long, long time.

Only one year prior my life had been completely different and from the outside it appeared that I had it all. I was married to my business partner and we had a beautiful young daughter. I had my elite card for triathlon and was a podium athlete. I represented my country on the National Duathlon Team, appeared daily on television, working with athletes and a few celebrities. I was the person who helped other people get what they wanted—fit, lean, healthy bodies—and here I was, falling apart.

One night in total desperation, a few days after we were locked out of our business, I got down on my knees and prayed. "God, if you will show me the way, I will do the work." I didn't know where the energy would come from because every minute of every day was a struggle; however, something deep within me knew that the only way was surrender and at this point resistance and trying to figure everything out was exhausting.

In June, with $300 in cash and a car full of possessions, I left my daughter with her father, and ended up living on my brother-in-law's sofa while I figured out how to piece a life together. I couldn't tell anyone that I was sick or I wouldn't get a job. I could have shamefully gone home to live with my dad but that was the last option and one that I wasn't willing to explore.

Thankfully my skills landed me a low-level management job for a major health club chain. It was really hard hiding my disease, but I didn't see another option. I had a child to provide for and I had to go on; it was that or completely give up, and that moment wouldn't come for a few more years.

I didn't tell anyone I was sick. I pushed and pushed. I ran my sales team and became the top producing department in a chain of four hundred and forty-four clubs. I continued to train for triathlons. I didn't tell my coach, my agent or even my family. From the outside it may not have been evident, but in those private moments while running, biking or swimming, I was internally damaged, disappointed and in a great deal of denial.

It is said that there are stages of grief when one is diagnosed with a disease. I have observed friends and family members who have gone through these stages, often starting with anger and then to denial, only to be followed by pushing back or completely giving up. In those days I wasn't ready to give up and I found that pretending I didn't have the disease seemed to serve me to a point – or so I thought, until my body started breaking down.

That summer, as I struggled in every area of my life, I also met the man I would marry. He would help me learn to trust again. He would stand by my side as my partner and my best friend. Most importantly, he would be there for the next three years as I drifted to the place where all I could selfishly think about every waking moment was taking my life so neither he, nor the kids, would have to watch as my body and my mind gave up.

By 2003, I had lost all hope. Chris and I were in survival mode. When I had a flare-up he would stand by helplessly as I spent days on the sofa. Sometimes we fought about money – specifically, the lack thereof – but I knew at the root of all of these arguments we were both angry and scared. This wasn't the life that either of us had signed up for.

In a last-ditch effort I began bargaining with God. My prayers went something like this: "God, if you want me to live, send me a sign," and, "God, I am so broken. Please fix me." I didn't have the energy to pray my prayer from three years ago; there was no more strength to draw on to let God know that I would do the work. As my body shut down I felt the only answer was take my life, as scary as that was.

On the day I planned to kill myself, my daughter ended up not going to camp because she wasn't feeling well. I remember so clearly that is was a bright, sunny Thursday in July, and it had taken me so long to muster the courage as the will to live left my body. At that time I didn't see it as any sort of sign; I simply put off taking my own life so I could be take care of my daughter.

That day was especially painful. The heat of the summer was causing greater fatigue and weakness. Looking into my sweet daughter's face I thought about what her life would be like without me, and conversely, what her life would be like watching me slowly die. At my lowest point, feeling stuck between two options, neither of which presented a happy outcome, I received a phone call – one that would dramatically alter the course of my life. Looking back I knew it was an answer to my prayers.

As much as we may hope that our lives will be a straight line, filled with obvious choices and high levels of clarity, this couldn't be farther from the truth; life is often filled with curves that alter our course, causing us to resist or allowing us to surrender. These seeming detours can ultimately take us to a place we could never have imagined. On this particular day, one decision led our entire family down a different path – one that changed my paradigm from a life of quiet desperation to one of having it all.

The person calling was a former client who was extremely well-versed in complementary medicine. She suggested I look at detoxifying my body – something that, even as a nutritionist, I had resisted. I was desperate and there was no more fight in my body. I wondered if this was God's intervention and after several phone calls, I decided to give this a try and once again put off the plan to take my life.

As I began to cleanse my body, other things in my life took on greater clarity. It was as though I had been living in black and white and suddenly the world was a vivid spectrum of color. I saw the love and desperation in my husband's face. I saw the trust in my children's eyes. I had been so selfish. I was deeply ashamed that I had thought the only option was to leave them.

As my energy improved, I took greater responsibility. I was not a victim. I could change my circumstances. I started to act as a rep for the nutritional company that produced the cleanse and we began to bring in more money. That extra money took off some of the financial pressure. We were no longer fighting as much.

Step by step, I worked on changing my circumstances. Every day I asked God to forgive me for having had those thoughts of suicide. Just moving in a different direction gave me hope and courage to take bigger and bolder steps. Eventually I became healthy and that health fuelled my marriage, my ability to parent and my capacity to dream, and gave me the energy to radically change our financial circumstances.

What I didn't know then, which is intensely apparent now, is that I could have chosen to *have it all*, even at my lowest point. Had I known that having it all was simply an attitude – one that can shift any life circumstance – and not a laundry list of material goods, I would never have contemplated taking my own life.

As we journey together through this book I want you to understand one thing right now: you already *have it all* to some degree. Like me, so many years ago, you just may not know it yet.

Taking Stock

"If you realized how powerful your thoughts are, you would never think a negative thought."

— Peace Pilgrim, *Advocate*

If I had really looked at my life when I was at my lowest point I would have realized that it wasn't as bad as I was making it out to be. Yes, I was extremely sick, in a tremendous amount of pain, had very little money and felt hopeless; however, had I not been feeling sorry for myself and acting the victim I would have seen that I did have much more than that I realized.

I had a wonderful partner. I had two beautiful children, and even though our son was presenting as autistic, he was healthy. I had a roof over my head. There was food to eat. We had clean water to drink. We also had the support system of Chris' parents and my father who lived nearby. Having now travelled, on several occasions, to Africa and Cambodia, seeing women who starve to death while holding infants in their arms, people wasting away from HIV and AIDS, children who are so emaciated that you can make out the lines of their organs, I now know that even then I had so much more than hundreds of millions of women on the planet.

As women we can often feel sorry for ourselves. We can overdramatize our circumstances. We can create a reality that feels hopeless. The truth is that no matter what, we all have more than we realize if we stop for a moment to take stock.

At the women's retreats we have run, we have historically partnered with a large women's drop-in center. Through this partnership I have met many extraordinary women going through tough times. Many of these women sleep in shelters. Some are moms, some grandmothers, and some have college degrees. Whether through drug or alcohol addiction, mental illness or simply through circumstance they come to this drop-in center in search of improving their lives.

I met one woman, forty-something with a beautiful smile that revealed several missing teeth, whom we will call Josephine, who had become a crack addict. At her lowest point she slit both her wrists. She hadn't seen her children in years. She spoke about life in the shelter system and the desperation of trying to make it to the shelter in time to get a hot meal and a warm bed. She shared her story of trading sex for drugs and the helplessness of living in a walking coma while sleeping on the street.

One day, Josephine heard from another woman about the drop-in center. She went initially to get a hot lunch. At the center she found other women, some sharing similar circumstances, who were taking computer classes, using art as therapy, learning how to read and so much more. There she also found her voice, and through the help of a social worker, joined the writing program.

Josephine got off the drugs and began counseling other women. She also began writing more and advocating for women to share their own stories. When I met Josephine I asked her what that tipping point moment was for her; when did she say "enough is enough"?

Her reply was that sometimes you have to get to a place where you hit rock bottom and even at that moment if you have a warm place to go for part of the day and someone who is fighting for you then you have it pretty good. What I realized is that this beautiful woman understood something that many women do not – when we take stock of what we have, we realize that we always have everything we need to take the next step.

Focus on What You Are Going To and Not What You are Going Through

"...I came to realize that God never shows us something we aren't ready to understand. Instead, He lets us see what we need to see, when we need to see it. He'll wait until our eyes and hearts are open to Him, and then when we're ready. He will plant our feet on the path that's best for us...but it's up to us to do the walking."

—Immaculee Ilibagiza, *Author*

Let me ask you a question – what do you have going for you in your life right now that you are not appreciating? Do you have at least one person who supports you? Do you have a roof over your head and a warm place to sleep? Do you have clean food to eat and water to drink? You have already set yourself apart.

As you read this, know that you can always have more in your life. You may have to work for it. You may have to make radical changes. It may not happen overnight. It may take months or even years. You may have to face what seem like insurmountable odds; however, the bottom line is that regardless of what is happening right now, you can *have it all* and it begins with shifting your mindset.

I once heard a sermon by Pastor Joel Osteen. He was delivering a message of hope that was centered upon the theme that in order to transcend our circumstances we must focus on what we are going to, or moving toward, and not what our present life is like right now. In other words, our current reality does not have to dictate our future outcome.

While in Malawi, Africa, I stopped by a bookstore to find something to read on the long plane ride home. I was drawn to the book *Left to Tell*, by Immaculée Ilibagiza, a story of a woman who survived the Rwandan genocide by seeking refuge, with seven other women, in the cramped bathroom of a local pastor.

During the ninety-one days of torturous concealment, Immaculée could hear the brigade of murderers calling her name outside the Pastor's home. With very little food, her weight plummeted and because of the filthy conditions of the bathroom, the women contracted scabies in addition to numerous open sores on their bodies.

Throughout, Immaculée continued to pray. She focused on not only surviving but living beyond what seemed to be a situation with only one possible outcome—death. Although all of her family had been slaughtered, with the exception of one brother studying abroad, Immaculée did not blame God, which would have been easy to do. Instead she kept her focus on the future as the uncertainty of war raged on.

When the war ended, Immaculée narrowly escaped death as she, along with the other women, sought asylum in a UN camp. As she continued to focus on what she wanted, her life transformed. Immaculée is now a published author, speaker, and mother, and continues to bring awareness to the ongoing healing required in Rwanda.

Imagine, for a moment, fleeing for your life, an execution squad at the door, spending a quarter of a year locked in a bathroom never knowing if today would be your last. Could you have this woman's faith? Could you focus forward? Even when it seemed like Immaculée had nothing, she knew she had it all in her heart and this is where the journey begins – not externally, with possessions and the trappings of apparent success; it begins within, knowing that we always can *have it all* because no matter what hurtful things another person does to us, no one can take away our soul.

The Four D's

"With clarity and certainty there can be no overwhelm." — Susan Sly

In this work we are going to journey through key aspects of your life. From your health to your relationships to your money—these words and exercises are intended to truly help you become the woman that you were Divinely created to be. Many women, and men, struggle with overwhelm. When there is too much to do it becomes too onerous and the tendency is to give up. It is for this reason that each chapter, and every step, ultimately comes down to the Four D's—**Decide**, **Define**, **Delegate**, **Delete** or **Dump**, and **Definitive Action**.

This chapter is centered on the initial step – simply making the decision. In each aspect of our lives there are decisions to make, and as women, we make thousands on a daily basis. From the clothes we choose, to the food we eat, to the actions we take, to the thoughts we think, we are decision-making machines.

Often faced with making decisions—not only for ourselves, but for others in our lives, such as our children, our partner, family members, colleagues and friends – we are often left with decision fatigue; to make one more decision can be exhausting even though it may be indeed the most important thing we do.

When I was diagnosed with MS, I made a decision that I was not going to be a victim. Like Montel Williams, the television host and MS champion, who proclaimed that he had MS and MS did not have him, I too decided that if this was the diagnosis then I was going to choose to look for alternatives to conventional care. I decided that I was going to live my life to the fullest. It was tough at times to live into this decision and I was close to giving up. However, some days, simply deciding to put one foot in front of the other or take more vitamins kept me going.

Our decisions create our reality and thus this first 'D' is imperative to each area we focus on. In each chapter there will be decisions to be made, some of which will be very exciting, while others may feel daunting. I suggest you simply allow yourself to decide that you want more and follow your heart through the words and exercises.

The second 'D' is all about defining what something means to us. In this chapter we will seek to create the definition of what it means to *have it all*, on our terms. In other chapters we will define personal health, wealth and rewarding relationships. These personal definitions will serve as our internal GPS.

The third 'D' is the step where we learn how to delegate, delete or dump something that is not serving us. To *have it all* means not doing it all and there are always ways in which we can simply, create breathing room and release those things which are not in alignment with our journey to living a more fulfilling and rich life.

The last 'D', definitive action, is where we move forward, taking the actions that will thrust us toward our dreams. Any new action can be temporarily uncomfortable, and yet once we repeat it, and it becomes a habit, we wonder how we lived without this way of being.

Using the Four D strategy will assist you as we work through the key aspects of your life. Furthermore, in Chapter Three, we will bring your life into greater balance using the *have it all* life pyramid—clarifying how to create a solid foundation which will serve as a launch pad to living the life of your dreams.

One thing I often say in seminars is that with clarity and certainty there can be no overwhelm. The goal is to live your *have it all* life without any overwhelm. As you journey through this book, I urge you to breathe, focus on one thing at a time and know, beyond a shadow of a doubt, that the same God that created all of the powerful, *have it all woman* through history also created you.

The Decision

"Like my mother, I was always saying, 'I'll fix my life one day.' It became clear when I saw her die without fulfilling her dreams that my time was now or maybe never."

—Liz Murray, *Speaker*

Elizabeth (Liz) Murray was born on September 23rd in the Bronx to two drug-addicted parents who would quickly spend any welfare payments on heroin and cocaine. To say that her life was hard would be an understatement. At one point, Liz and her sister split a tube of toothpaste because they were desperate for something to eat. When they were hungry, they would eat ice cubes to simulate the experience of chewing on food.

It hadn't always been this way. Liz's parents had once been hippies and then became regulars on the Disco scene. A mild drug habit turned into a raging one that led to the demise of the family. Even when the family was at the lowest point, Liz's mother would continue to say, "Things are going to get better." Liz carried this mantra through as her life began to unravel.

As a child she was infrequent to school and when she did show up she was often lice-ridden and severely malnourished. By the age of fifteen, Liz's mother died and her father was moved to a homeless shelter. Liz was now officially living on the streets full-time. Her sister found refuge on a friend's sofa.

Liz made a decision to turn her life around and entered high school. Despite not having regularly attended school, she graduated in just two years and went on to receive a full scholarship to Harvard. It was Liz's courageous decision to not be a victim of circumstance that has her now living an entirely different life as a best-selling author and motivational speaker.

Like Liz, you may be going through some tough times. You may be close to financial devastation or relying on a shelter system. Perhaps, financially things are all right, but your health is poor or you are on the verge of an emotional breakdown. Take courage in Liz's story and make a decision right now, that no matter what, you are going to turn things around and create a new, more positive, outcome for yourself.

The Definition

"A woman is the full circle. Within her is the power to create, nurture, and transform."

— Diane Mariechild, *Author*

In Immaculée's story we see a woman who, like the phoenix, rises from the ashes, taking full flight and creating a *have it all* life. As a public figure committed to building awareness of the ongoing healing in Rwanda, and a mother and wife in good health, Immaculée has it all. For this courageous woman the journey began in her mind, surviving in the filthy bathroom, dreaming day after day about what her life would be.

To *have it all*, we must first define it for ourselves. This esoteric notion that we must live into someone else's ideal will only serve to cause us pain, frustration, resentment and inevitably frustration. Having it all is not reflected by status symbols; it is purely about the journey within, which creates a launch pad for our outer world to begin reflecting our inner world.

Ultimately having it all is to achieve personal fulfillment in three key areas: health, relationships and money. Within those parameters come personal definitions. For example, for some being healthy may mean simply maintaining an appropriate weight, while for others it may mean shaving time off a personal best for the marathon.

In terms of relationships, a woman who has been widowed, losing her longtime love, may define fulfilling relationships as those with her children or grandchildren, while the single woman, looking for love, may define it as finding the perfect partner.

Lastly, when it comes to money, some women may define success as being able to pay bills with ease, while others may be looking to fuel a lifestyle of travel and philanthropy. Essentially, within the three key tenets of having it all, lie subjective, wide-ranging definitions.

When we see a woman driving a luxury car, carrying the latest Louis Vuitton handbag, looking immaculate in perfectly fitted clothing, we cannot automatically assume that she has it all. She could be struggling through a painful divorce, dealing with an illness of a family member or fighting personal addictions. The truth is that having it all cannot be immediately surmised simply by what we see on the outside; each and every woman has her own story and although externally may seem to be living a *have it all* life, internally she may be struggling.

The goal of this book is to assist you in becoming a *have it all woman* – to create a life in which there is no more striving for external rewards. You may already have one, or more, or the key factors – the health or the fulfilling relationship or the money to fuel your personal dreams – or none at all. The wonderful thing is that we can all grow, we can always create more in our lives and no matter where you are right now, you can *have it all.*

Delete It! Other People's Perspectives Do Not Have to Shape Our Reality

"No one can make you feel inferior without your consent."

— Eleanor Roosevelt, *First Lady*

Oprah Gail Winfrey was born into poverty in rural Mississippi to a single teenage mother on January 29th, 1954. At age nine, Oprah was raped and by age fourteen she gave birth to a son who later died in infancy. To say that Oprah's early life was hard would be an understatement.

As a child she was told that she was ugly and would never amount to anything. She was shuffled around, abused and neglected. Many people had opinions about Oprah and she would go on to design her own life, become the most powerful woman in media, transform generations, and ultimately, absolutely not live into anyone else's notion of who or what Oprah was. She defined her own worth.

Other people's perspectives of our lives are often interesting things, and something we can either use to contribute to our power, or dwell on as a mechanism to take us out of the gain. Eleanor Roosevelt once said, "The good opinion of others is none of my business." Essentially, like Oprah, she simply decided to live her life giving little heed of what other people were saying. To truly *have it all*, you are going to have to let go of the opinions of others unless you can use those to help you become the powerful, *have it all woman*, you are destined to be.

Over time I have been called a variety of things: loving, edgy, beautiful, angry, peaceful, tough, powerful, compassionate, genuine, honest, emotional, aggressive, competitive, diplomatic, a leader, a follower, a procrastinator, fat, thin, ugly, dark, light, tall, short, round, pudgy, and the list goes on and on. Yes, I have even been called a bitch. So there you have it: I either have multiple personalities, or I am a cross-section of just about every woman on the planet.

At times, I have allowed people's criticism to be the cause of some obsession, though inherently the thing I have learned is that anyone who is being hurtful is someone who is hurting themselves in some way. Once we decide that we can *have it all*, we may be faced with criticism and often from those closest to us. It is important to remember that we will have critics no matter what we do in life and living for our critics is a surefire way to deter us from any potential happiness.

Garner strength from Oprah's story. Know that YOU create your life. Let go of the opinion of anyone else because that is a surefire way to give away your power. You can *have it all*, you can design a life where you play bigger than you could have ever imagined and it simply begins within; no one else's opinion has influence over you unless you decide to allow it.

Take Definitive Action

In this chapter, as we focus simply on making a decision and creating a definition for what having it all means in our own lives, know that you are already taking definitive action; you are moving toward the fulfilled, powerful, incredible woman you were Divinely destined to be. At the end of this chapter is an exercise that will assist you in gaining even further perspective and it is absolutely encouraged that you take some time to do it before moving on to the next area of focus.

Lastly – Our Past Does Not Have to Dictate our Future

"You only see the glory, you don't know the story." — Natalie Cole, *Singer*

Like Liz Murray, I grew up with a highly educated drug- and alcohol-addicted mother. When I was three years old, my mother kidnapped me in her effort to assume parental responsibility for me. That attempt at parenting, however, lacked continuity because of her struggles with addictions to prescription medication, which she conveniently obtained in her work as a registered nurse.

For years, my mother was a somewhat high-functioning addict; the outside world was largely not aware of her ongoing battle. Like many addicts, my mother's compulsions did not stop at only one vice. She was a chronic chain smoker – something that caused me to be born with smoker's lungs and immediately placed in an oxygen tent – and addicted to religion, something that took her from Catholicism to the Pentecostal Church to the Mormons and beyond.

As a child, I was not allowed to wear pants because my mother considered them satanic. There were no story books, only the Bible and approved Church readings. There were no movies or television shows, as all of these things were also "from Satan." My weekends were spent at tent revivals and my evenings on buses going to and from Church.

When my mother got paid she would immediately buy cartons of cigarettes, stuffed animals for me, and groceries, which consisted of hot dogs and Kraft dinner. Within a few days, the groceries and the cigarettes would run out. My mother would pick up cigarette butts from the ground and re-smoke them. I remember once being so hungry that I took Monopoly money to the grocery store in an attempt to buy food. I was so embarrassed when the cashier laughed at me.

My mother often worked the night shift and would leave me alone. I wore a key around my neck on a shoestring. From the age of four I was a "latch-key" kid. When questioned by my father, who lived approximately a thousand miles away, she vehemently denied any wrongdoing.

At night I would go into our front hall closet, with my pillow and teddy bear, and surround myself with boxes and other paraphernalia. I was terrified. I would scream and cry for my mother and once, when the landlord came after hearing my cries, I refused to let him in knowing that my mother would get in trouble. The terror also came from the unknown, as my mother liked to continuously inform me that "Satan will come and take you if you are bad."

Even as a child I was fully aware that the environment I was living in was not healthy. I pleaded with my mom to let me live with my dad; she refused to let me go. By the time I was eight years old, I began to assert my power. For three days I stopped eating and informed my mother that I would not eat, go to school or conform in any way until I could go and live with my father. She finally relented.

Going to live with my father, who ran a restaurant with my grandmother, was like a breath of fresh air and it literally was – the polar opposite of the closed-in, suffocative, smoke-filled apartment I had lived in; neither my father nor my grandmother smoked. Instead of careless neglect there were enforced bedtimes, healthy meals and Saturdays spent going on adventures with my dad. Where there had been no discipline, there was now order. Although, like many children who had never experienced a "firm hand," I initially rebelled, and today, I thank God that I was able to come to live with my dad.

It has taken a long time, and a tremendous amount of work, to be able to forgive my mother. I love her; however, that does not mean that I agree with her choices. I accept what happened – the abuse and neglect – not as something that was once an anvil around my neck but as a beautiful reminder of the contrast of raising a child in a loving, positive home as opposed to the home of an addict.

My mother's lifelong struggles with addictions to alcohol and prescription medication have caused her to be in and out of my life. I have friends who have become sober and I have friends who have parents, children or partners that are addicts and it is one of the toughest things to deal with – to not know what kind of person you are going to find when you walk in the door. Living with an addict is hard, plain and simple.

I had thought that it was her addictions that caused her erratic behavior. At times my mother would go missing and then we would receive a call from a hospital or the police. At times she would be sweet and extremely loving and then she would become aggressive, only to deny the behavior later on. Although I love my mother, I had to create a boundary for my children. Nana was unpredictable and I couldn't expose them to her strange behaviors.

Honestly, I wrestled with my feelings about my mom. She conveniently didn't remember the abuse from my childhood or passing out for days. She didn't recall calling me and swearing; instead she told me that it was someone impersonating her. She would also tell me that she had been robbed of thousands of dollars that she didn't have or that the mafia was trying to kill her. Sadly, despite counseling, I longed for her to be different and silently envied women who appeared to have healthy relationships with their own mothers.

At the advice of a therapist, I distanced myself to create my own healthy boundary, though I wrestled with guilt. Our relationship was relegated to writing letters and occasional visits in public places, such as a Starbucks, that would allow me to feel safe.

In 2009 I received a call from a doctor who was treating her and, after 36 years, was told that my mother is schizophrenic and has borderline personality disorder. I cannot begin to explain what a relief it was to find out that her unusual behavior was not just in my mind.

So here I am – just Susan, the child of a schizophrenic addict. Like many women, I have been abused, I have had disappointments, I have longed for my life to be different and I have begged, on my knees, to be "like everyone else." Like Liz Murray, I have chosen not to let my past define me but to refine me and I encourage you to do the same. I know you may be hurting and you may have shielded much of your pain from the world, only to cause you heartbreak, sorrow, regret, anguish and perhaps bitterness. Let it go and please know that you can become the beautiful swan, you can design your life and you can absolutely *have it all* because above all else you are created from God; there is no power greater than the infinite potential of The Divine.

Four D's of Beginning Your Journey

Decide: Repeat this affirmation: "I can truly *have it all.*"

Define It: Create a definition of what *have it all* means to you.

Delete It: Let go of anyone else's opinions of your life.

Definitive Action: Write your one-year *have it all* vision letter.

Have It All Affirmation

I choose to live a have it all life.

- *HAVE IT ALL WOMAN* EMPOWERMENT EXERCISE -

A Letter to Myself

The following exercise is designed to help you set your GPS. In order to *have it all*, we must define it for ourselves. This will assist you in focusing forward.

Write a letter to yourself and date it one year from today. In the letter describe how your life is next year, as though it has already happened. Imagine that anything is possible—that you can truly be, do and have anything you dream. Include your health, your relationships and your finances. Do not leave out one detail.

CHAPTER TWO

Step 2: Creating a Clearing in Your Life

"The roughest road often leads to the top."

— Christina Aguilera, *Musician*

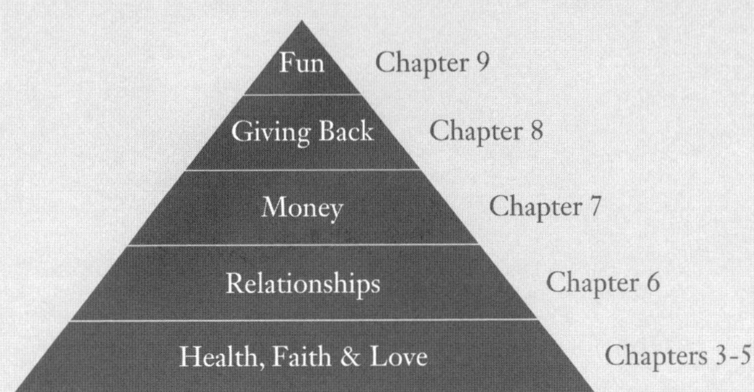

CHAPTER TWO

Step 2: Creating a Clearning in Your Life

The Decision to Clean It Up

"I long, as does every human being, to be at home wherever I find myself."

— Maya Angelou, *Poet, Author*

In every woman's life there are a series of events chronicled by possessions. We have letters from past lovers, the stuffed animal won at the fair, clothes that no longer fit and an entire lifetime of memories documented by stuff. Even those of us who feel that we are not in the category of "pack rat" undoubtedly have things that we can part with. To be a *have it all woman*, we must be able to create the clearing of the past in order to make room for the abundance of the future.

Sometimes parts of our lives feel "stuck." We feel suffocated, frustrated and downright out of control. Often we cannot pinpoint exactly what is going on. We look to ourselves, yet the answer is not obvious. The truth is that something as simple as purging the clutter can create breathing space.

In 2000, when I lost my business, my home, my money and all of my possessions save what could fit in my rented car, that experience became what I refer to as "the great purge." It was easy not to get attached to things when there was nothing to get attached to. I realized that I had defined my life by my possessions and not by who I was on the inside. From that time on, I have always cleared the clutter in my life because I have released attachment to material objects, knowing full well that they have only the meaning we give to them.

Of course I like my shoes, handbags and jewelry; however, they do not define me and nor do yours define you. The *have it all woman* may choose to have beautiful things, but they do not control her. Regardless of what is going on in a woman's life, at one time or another, it is fun to dress up and feel sexy. Shoes, dresses, great jewelry or even an amazing hair cut can boost our confidence. All of these material trappings, however, pale in comparison to the beauty that is within.

Selling Sex for Shoes

"In too many instances, the march to globalization has also meant the marginalization of women and girls. And that must change."

— Hillary Clinton, *Former Secretary of State*

One of my areas of philanthropic focus has been raising funds for a trauma centre in Cambodia. We have partnered with World Vision, one of the largest aid organizations in the world. The centre is a safe house for girls who have been sold into brothels, raped and molested. I have traveled to Cambodia, a country of beauty beyond measure with exceptionally resilient people, and am extremely comfortable in "the field." The field can mean human and animal sewage, people living under a tin roof with four posts, or playing soccer with boys in a field, uncertain as to whether or not it has been swept for landmines, with all of the above.

It has been heart-wrenching to come to hear the stories of how these children have come to be trafficked. Some were sold to brothels for their virginity. One girl's mother sold her to the brothel to pay for her gambling debts. Other girls went to the brothels, selling their bodies simply to buy expensive clothes, shoes and make-up; they went voluntarily because they associated these material goods with greater self-worth.

Some women marry into money because they associate living in a large home, driving a luxury car and carrying a Birkin bag with happiness, only to find that the latest bag, the off-the-runway outfit or the newest gadget only serves to temporarily provide a rush that doesn't even begin to quench the emptiness inside. Other women will spend their paycheck or max out their credit cards like the lovable Carrie Bradshaw in Sex In The City, in order to have the latest designer shoes. To be a slave to possessions will ultimately only serve to create a cycle of dependency – one that limits our ability to truly be free. These women may not be selling sex for shoes, but they are selling a piece of themselves.

As we begin to release excess in our lives and let go of the notion that our self-worth is defined by our purse or shoes, we begin to release any dependency on the material and truly step into our own power. Should we choose to purchase something that we like, then we do so from a place of knowing that we can afford it, we do not need it, and that although we may relish the experience of driving the car, carrying the bag or wearing the shoes, this in no way is necessary for our happiness.

The Fundamental Needs

"If you ask people what they've always wanted to do, most people haven't done it. That breaks my heart." —Angelina Jolie, *Actress*

Travelling to Guatemala and other parts of the world where children lack adequate shelter, education, health and safety has provided wonderful perspective. In the field all that is required are my hiking boots, simple pants, t-shirts, a back pack and notebook. Connecting with people who have survived genocides, rape, conquest and brutal atrocities provides contrast to everyday Western life. In these parts of the world, simple needs such as clean water, food, shelter and safety are luxuries – ones that we so often take for granted.

Some of the most incredible and inspiring women I have ever met were encountered in poor, rural areas in Cambodia and Africa. On one trip I met a group of women, stricken by HIV, who were making bamboo mats to sell for money to buy medications. I took a turn with the giant machete attempting to peel the bamboo and we all had a great laugh. Despite being sick, poor and outcast from their village, these women were so strong, so powerful and so beautiful. To these women having it all simply meant money to buy medications, shelter, food for their families and the ability to send their children to school; this is what brought happiness and fulfillment.

Dr. Abraham Maslow, the founder of the humanist movement, wrote a paper entitled The Hierarchy of Needs. In his work Dr. Maslow proposed that once our physiological needs are met, including breathing, food, water, and sleep, we are then in a position to ascend to a higher level of purpose in our lives. In the next level of the hierarchy, safety was to be obtained and once this was achieved then one could work toward love, fulfillment, and self-actualization. Based on Dr. Maslow's work, one could ascertain that any woman who has her physiological needs met, is safe, and has love, does indeed truly *have it all.*

Meeting women who can survive—and even thrive—on very little yields incredible perspective. In your own life you may know women who are balanced and fulfilled with seemingly little attachment to the material because they fully understand what is important. The *have it all woman* is able to look at her life objectively from the vantage point of understanding what is truly important and what is simply something that is nice to have.

At the end of the day we can survive, and perhaps even thrive, with much less than we think we can. I pray that you do not have to go through a major life catastrophe to fully appreciate that we require much less than we likely realize, and that be releasing the excess from our lives we send a clear signal that we are indeed ready to receive more.

An exercise from A Course in Miracles asks us to look around the room and repeat, "nothing I see in this room means anything." Of course it may feel odd or you may find resistance as you look at objects such as your dresser, your night stand, your desk, your computer or whatever it is and recite this lesson. Eventually, when repeated, you find that you truly see that every material object you possess only has the meaning you give it and once you release all meaning you release the stranglehold of your possessions. In doing this you take back your power as many women work, strive and force themselves to do things they know cause pain because they live in fear of losing their possessions or of judgment of how they will be categorized without them.

Would You Pay $1 Per Pound?

"Optimism is the faith that leads to achievement. Nothing can be done without hope and confidence." — Helen Keller, *Advocate*

Take a moment to consider what is essential to your day-to-day existence and what is not. Where do you have excess? Many women look around and see areas of clutter. Have you ever looked in your purse and found it overflowing with unfiled receipts, make-up, loose change, papers, or diaper wipes? Have you opened your closet only to find it full of clothes that no longer fit? Do you have a pile of old magazines that you know you will never read? What does your car look like inside? Do you have a junk drawer, or two, or three?

There are many places around our homes, and in our lives, to amass clutter. Whether you realize it or not, this clutter is most likely affecting your income, relationships, health and everything around you. If you have no room to move, you cannot have space to attract and create.

According to the website Zillow.com the average cost of moving a household, including taxes, boxes and extras is approximately $1/per pound. As you look around your home ask yourself if you would pay $1/per pound to move something. If the answer is "no," then ask yourself, could you let that thing go?

We all have excess. We all can simplify. There are always more things we can let go of to create greater freedom in our lives. In this chapter we will work to create a clearing, release surplus and design a life into which we have much more room for abundance to flow.

A Place for Abundance to Flow

"God answers sharp and sudden on some prayers, And thrusts the thing we have prayed for in our face, A gauntlet with a gift in it."

— Elizabeth Barrett Browning, *Poet*

When there is a place for abundance to flow, you will easily attract it. Have you ever moved into a new home and realized that there was more space than you had stuff to fill? How long was it before those empty spaces filled up with things? It doesn't take long.

For most women, we get a great deal of comfort from our possessions. Some of us even use them to feel secure. I have worked with many clients who judge their worth by the clothes they wear and the car they drive. Hey, I am not saying there is anything wrong with beautiful clothing or a high-end car. These things, however, are not a measure of your value. Your value is determined by your spirit.

When we are surrounded by a mess, other parts of our life suffer. When we have parts of our home that are cluttered, unconsciously, we are sending a message to the world that we have no room to receive more. When we have junk piling up, our thoughts are directed there as opposed to seeking opportunities to get what we want and so rightly deserve. Releasing clutter is something that is easily done, and can yield the greatest rewards.

Clutter can also come in the form of past events or emotions that we are not clearing. Focusing energy on events or people who no longer serve us creates a type of mental litter, if you will, that prevents us from moving forward into something more powerful. Inherently a cluttered environment is so often a reflection of a cluttered mind. By removing our environmental clutter we ultimately begin to de-clutter our mind.

Define Your Uncluttered Life

"Even the wildest dreams have to start somewhere. Allow yourself the time and space to let your mind wander and your imagination fly."

— Oprah Winfrey, *Media Personality*

Take a moment to imagine your life without clutter or chaos. Visualize what life would be like if everything had order, you knew exactly where every item was, your closet was perfectly arranged, every room in flow, every aspect of your life with breathing room to attract more. How would it feel? What if life became easier simply because it was uncluttered?

Generally speaking, we all have at least one area that is not organized or in flow.

It could be a home office, your bedroom, a playroom, a den, your garage or your kitchen. Interestingly enough, that one area is often associated with an aspect of our life that doesn't feel good, as though something is not quite right. For example, if your bedroom is a mess perhaps your relationship is not the greatest. If your home office is disorganized perhaps your finances are chaotic.

For many years I have taught a course called Organize Your Life. During the first class, I ask students to consider their top life priority. For some it may be to increase the amount of money coming into their household; for others it may be to heal the relationship with their partner or attract their ideal partner. For others still it may be to improve their health. Time after time, we see that the area of the home associated with the objective is generally cluttered and chaotic. This is the first area they are asked to clean up.

What happens, time and time again, is that as the students clear the clutter in their home, "magical" things begin to happen. Stubborn weight is suddenly released. Money automatically shows up. A relationship that has been tense is quickly healed. It happens almost overnight and many students ask themselves why they hadn't taken action before.

I once had a student who was having challenges with her marriage. She and her husband hadn't made love in months. It seemed as though every day there was a new argument. From ideas about how to raise the kids to the finances, each topic seemed to elicit a fight.

I asked my student to describe her bedroom. "I am embarrassed," she said shyly. "Trust me," I implored, "I want to help."

She shared how her bedroom had become an extension of the laundry room. There were clothes stacked on the treadmill, piled on the floor and baskets upon baskets of garments waiting to be folded. When I asked her how it felt to her she confessed that she experienced a sense of suffocation every time she entered the room. I gently suggested that perhaps her husband felt the same way and that it was time to clean it up.

My student spent an entire weekend dealing with the clothes. She donated some to worthwhile charities, she put away the clothes that were still in use and stored those items that were seasonal. By Sunday night, the room was free of clutter and both she and her husband felt renewed. That night they made love. They went on to have fewer and fewer arguments, hardly fighting at all. Simply organizing her bedroom, the room associated with her top priority, shifted the chaos which allowed both her and her husband to feel more relaxed and open.

Ask yourself what is really important in your life right now. What needs to be dealt with? Is there a monkey on your back? Are there back taxes? Do you have creditors at your door? Is your relationship in turmoil? Do you have a health concern? Make a decision to clean up the area associated with your top priority allowing the notion to take root that perhaps, like my student, the simple act of releasing clutter can have massive impact in your life.

Kate's Closet

"I know God won't give me anything I can't handle. I just wish he didn't trust me so much." —Mother Teresa

I had a client who had closets, bins and bags full of clothes that she no longer wore. To make matters worse, some of them still had their tags on. Kate (not her real name) was also frustrated in her business. She had started a marketing venture and was having difficulty attracting customers. When she did find a new customer they often wouldn't repeat buy.

Kate's life was stagnating in other areas. Her relationships were short-lived. She had a habit of attracting the wrong kind of man. She would find someone with great chemistry, fall in love and inevitably the relationship would become smothering. In the arena of romance, Kate often felt suffocated.

Kate's health was also a factor. She would lose ten pounds and gain ten pounds back. She felt disenchanted with her body. She would constantly get sinus infections and feel aches in her joints. Kate's body was congested.

In one of our first sessions I asked Kate to describe her surroundings. I knew the answer even before she gave it. Room after room was loaded with papers, clothes, knick knacks. Kate even had taxes she hadn't filed. Every room was so full that she wasn't able to move in some of them.

She had boxes of old training materials from former companies. She had bags full of books that she hadn't read. Her office was a disaster. I couldn't even find the phone.

One day I asked Kate how she felt in her home. She said that she loved it and that it felt safe. By the same token she was ashamed to have people over lest they might see the real woman, the one with the boxes and bags of unopened and unused things. I knew that Kate was using material goods to create a false sense of security.

Little by little, with my help, Kate began to purge her excess clothes. She also began to donate books, household items and other things to charities in need. As this happened her body began to respond. She was breathing easier, and she became leaner. She was also feeling lighter.

After one week of deliberate purging she attracted some strong leaders into her enterprise. Her business began to take on a life of its own. She began attracting with ease. Even her relationships improved. Kate went from being broke to being a multiple six-figure earner and it all started with the purge.

Delegate – Enlist Some Help

"Never interrupt someone doing something you said couldn't be done."

— Amelia Earhart, *Pilot*

I once had a student, whom we will call Anna. Anna lamented on many occasions how little money she had. From our coaching sessions I knew that Anna's life was chaos. She often was late, couldn't find things, and her personal life was a mess. She complained that her family was falling apart. When I asked her when the last time was that she, her husband, and kids had gone out to do something fun was, she once again expressed that it had been a long time because they could not afford it.

Fortunately Anna was extremely coachable. I put her through the following exercise and, if you have children at home, this is something I suggest you do as well. It is fun, effective and brings the entire family together collectively with a common goal. If you live by yourself or with a partner, you can also do this exercise.

In this exercise you clear a one- to two-hour period of time. The objective is to find money, gift cards, gift certificates and coupons – anything that has immediate financial value. Generally nothing is off-limits save perhaps your wallet. The sofa cushions, the car, the junk drawer and basically everywhere are potential treasure troves of unrealized potential. Set up a central location to deposit the bounty and see what happens.

In Anna's case the family "found" $476 worth of cash, gift cards and other miscellaneous discount certificates. Anna used a small part of the money to make a payment on a credit card and the rest funded a family adventure day that included a dinner out and an IMAX movie. They had an incredible time.

Like Anna, you may be in a situation where the clutter is masking hidden treasures. By setting the intention to clean things up, and enlisting the help of others in your household, you may also find that you have cash, gift cards and other items you didn't remember were there.

Regardless of your situation, never be afraid to ask for help. Chances are you know some people who love to tidy up and organize. Having a friend who is ruthless about getting rid of things can be helpful especially if you are struggling to let go. Furthermore, you may also wish to "divide and conquer" by delegating certain areas of the house to family members and then offering a reward once the task is accomplished.

The Million-Dollar Garage Sale

"I'll try anything once, twice if I like it, three times to make sure."

— Mae West, *Performer*

My friends Robin and Stryker were broke. Robin had been let go from a company where she was earning a six-figure income and was unable to find something comparable. As their savings wound down things got so bad that they couldn't make their mortgage payment. They decided to have a garage sale.

They worked hard at the sale and it yielded enough money to make the payment. At the same time, Robin's friend approached her with a business opportunity. Robin's initial investment could potentially turn into a massive long-term residual income. After reviewing the company, Robin became excited and she made a tough decision. She decided to use the mortgage money to invest in the business.

Needless to say, things were stressful, but Robin and Stryker's faith, determination and work ethic caused them to turn that initial investment into over a million dollars within a few short years. Today, their lives are entirely different. Robin's message is that she doesn't encourage people to do the same thing, but she always lets people know that where there is a will, there is a way.

Your Top Ten

"I hate housework! You make the beds, you do the dishes and six months later you have to start all over again." —Joan Rivers, *Comedian*

Another wonderful exercise to do is to take a clipboard and a blank piece of paper and walk around your house. List everything that is bothering you. It could be a messy garage, it could be a stain on the carpet; it could be boxes in the basement or children's clothing that no longer fit. Whatever it is, the list is important. Whether you realize it or not, these little annoyances are affecting your energy and your productivity.

When you walk around your home and see something that bothers you, immediately there is a negative emotion. There is usually some self talk that goes like this, "I need to fix..." or "I need to clean up..." and we do this day after day. Eventually our own sense of self worth is affected because we feel inadequate or overwhelmed because of the build up of tasks that we must complete. I want you to know that every time you see that crooked picture, the chip in the paint or whatever it is...you are affected.

A friend of mine once went on a goodwill mission to Mexico. He took all of his "good" old clothes out of his closet and his family did the same. I had shared with him the notion that when we create a clearing, something better flows to it, and he was absolutely ready. My friend and his family took their clothing and several other items to an orphanage. People were so grateful to be receiving "new" clothes. When my friend returned, a colleague happened to give him all of his barely used Armani, Brioni and Zenga designer clothing. In creating the clearing in his closet, my friend had created a space for abundance to flow.

As you look at your surroundings what do you see? Is there one cushion that needs repair? Is there an old pair of shoes you will never wear? Are there small home projects that could be completed yet remain undone? Everyone has a list of things that require attention. The longer you let them go, the bigger the list.

Many of the little jobs that need doing are just that – little jobs. Listing them and putting them in order of importance is the first step to finding some peace. As you walk around your home, write down all of the areas that need addressing. It doesn't matter how many you have, just that each one is on your list. Whatever is bothering you is likely bothering everyone else in your home.

The Power of Five

"Analyzing the problem is vital. It's the only way you're going to arrive at the right thing to do." — Vanessa Redgrave, *Actor*

On Sunday nights, Chris, the kids and myself all go around and find five things to throw out. It may be old notices from school, junk mail, bits of crayon or anything at all which is of no use to us or anyone else. This process is powerful because we are teaching our children not to hold on to clutter. It also allows us to start off Monday with a clearing where we are not looking at all of the miscellaneous "bits of stuff" around the house.

Could you create a new habit in your home? Could you take one day where everyone is encouraged to purge clutter? Imagine the possibilities? What would your life look like if everyone just simply took responsibility for their own mess? It can be awesome if you commit.

When we started the process, the kids were not that focused. After several weeks in a row they knew that if Chris or I declared it time to get rid of five things, it was time to act. Having developed the habit, they also feel empowered because they – not we – decide what is important. As a mother it can be heart-wrenching trying to choose between one week's macaroni art and another week's finger painting. My children connect to what they feel is worth keeping and it has taught me a lot about life through their eyes.

Even if you are on your own, establish a “get rid of five things” night once every week. Get rid of anything that no longer serves you. Ask yourself, “If I were to move, would I take this with me?” If the answer is “no,” then get rid of it. With dedication to the process, you will soon be living a life where abundance has a place to flow.

The Power of Five can be used in any area of your home. In making a decision what to purge you can ask yourself, “Have I used this in the last five years?” If not then purge it. Of course you may want to make exceptions for things like wedding gowns and other heirlooms. Ask yourself if you will use this item five years from now. If the answer is “no,” then toss it.

If you are going to be using something within the next five months then keep it out. If you do not need it until after five months from now, put it away; a great example of such things are winter coats, decorations and other seasonal items.

One of our students, Christine, became so masterful at creating a clearing using these principles that she actually found $17,000 in receipts that led to a tax refund of the same amount! Another student, a mom of four, uses this principle anytime she walks into a room. She asks herself, “What five things can I recycle, pitch or put away right now?” Dealing with only five things at a time is not overwhelming and generates a genuine sense of accomplishment.

What Do I Do With This Stuff?

"Everything is interconnected. It's all about living a healthier and happier life and loving life, and making that your focus."

— Daryl Hannah, *Actor*

The biggest thing to understand is that someone may need your things more than you do. There are so many worthwhile causes: from single mothers' programs to disaster relief. Personally, I never sell anything. I firmly believe that when you give, you receive tenfold. I give away all of my things with love.

As you are sorting stuff, divide it into piles. Take one pile and allocate those items to either friends or family who may need them. I have nephews who love my son's hand-me-down clothes. A.J. grows so fast that he barely wears something one or two times before it is too small. I invest in quality clothing, so why not pass it on someone in my family?

I had one friend who, due to some unfortunate events, could not afford to buy her children back-to-school clothing. I selected some great things and took them over. She was overcome with gratitude and her kids absolutely loved the clothes.

Due to speaking and traveling engagements I try to keep my wardrobe fresh. I have many classic pieces, but things that are trendier tend to be good for a select number of appearances. I also donate business clothing to women's shelters where wonderful ladies are trying to create a new life.

For quality toys, many women's shelters, Sunday schools, preschools and daycares can benefit from these items. We teach our children that other children do not have what we have. Toys are merely a dream for a child in a home where food, shelter and clothing are the chief concerns. Those toys sitting in your basement can bring a big smile to the face of a child.

A second unused set of dishes and other kitchen paraphernalia can be donated to a college student. The Salvation Army or a local church may also know of a family in need. When we donate dishes, cutlery and other kitchen items, we make sure there is at least a matching pair or set. People just starting out or rebuilding their lives will get the best use out of your excess kitchen items.

For furniture and just about anything else, organizations such as Goodwill or the Salvation Army can assist you. There are many families touched by tragedy who cannot afford to furnish their apartment or home. In our home, we have a list of different agencies that can receive our things. Many organizations will actually come to your home and pick up things.

Lastly, before you donate something, clean it up. If it is clothing then wash and fold it nicely. If it is furniture, then clean that up too. When you prepare to purge, do so with love. Know that someone out there needs these things more than you do, and be willing to let them go.

Take Action

"Nobody can make you feel inferior without your permission."

— Eleanor Roosevelt, *First Lady*

Undoubtedly you have heard the expression that the only way to eat an elephant is one bite at a time. If you are living in clutter and chaos then the only way to deal with it is one room at a time. The faster you begin to clear the clutter, the faster greater abundance will show up in your life. Use the following action steps and get started now. Once you have created a clearing you are ready for the next step which will assist you in building a solid foundation for creating your *have it all* life.

Clutter Clearing Tips:

1. Start With the Area Associated with Your Top Priority. For example, if you have immediate financial needs, then begin with your home office area. If your health is poor, begin with your kitchen. If you are not sleeping, begin with your bedroom.
2. Enlist Help. Ask friends and family members to assist. If you can afford to do so, hire a professional organizer.

3. Make a List of Your Top 10. What are the top ten things that are bothering you? Is there chipped paint that annoys you? A torn cushion? A desk top that you cannot see? Take action on your top 10 once you have cleared the room associated with your number-one priority.
4. Use the 5 Principle. Ask yourself – have you used this in the last five years? Will you use this in the next five years? If the answer is "no," then it absolutely must go unless there is some degree of sentiment such as a wedding dress. Will you use this in the next five months? If "no," you could toss it or store it. For example, seasonal goods such as a skis and snowboards could be stored. Will you use this in the next five weeks? If "yes," then you may wish to keep it somewhere handy that you can easily find it. Will you use this in the next five days? Keep it within sight. Will you use it in the next five hours? Then have it ready.
5. Donate With Love. Find a shelter, daycare or somewhere to donate your surplus that can truly benefit.

Use the Four-D Principle to Create a Clearing

Decide to create a clearing in your life for abundance to flow.

Define what your life looks like "clutter-free."

Dump anything that is excess and does not serve you using the Five Principle.

Delegate some of your purging. Do you have a child, partner or friend who would happily assist you?

Definitive Action: donate any clothes that no longer fit, items that you do not use or anything that sends mixed messages, such as old love letters. Continue to purge items on a weekly basis.

Have It All Affirmation

My life has plenty of breathing space.

- *HAVE IT ALL WOMAN* EMPOWERMENT EXERCISE -

Describe Your Space

Write a description of what your home looks like with ample breathing space. Write it as though you are a realtor giving a virtual tour. For example, you might say, "The closet area is perfectly arranged. All of the clothes are beautifully color-blocked. The purses and shoes are all aligned. Walking into this closet feels like entering a showroom..." Write about as many rooms as possible.

CHAPTER THREE

Step 3: Creating Abundant Health

"Be faithful in small things because it is in them that your strength lies."

— Mother Teresa

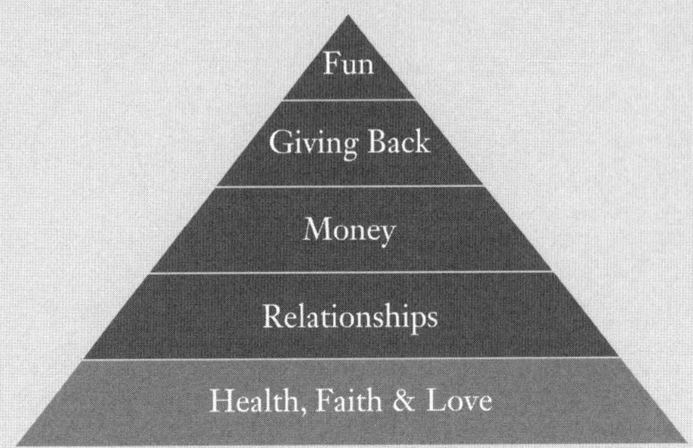

CHAPTER THREE

Step 3: Creating Abundant Health

Can a Pyramid Balance on Its Tip?

"A sure way to lose happiness, I found, is to want it at the expense of everything else." — Bette Davis, *Actress*

Think, for a moment, about a pyramid. It is solid in structure and sits upon a large foundation. The pyramids of the world have stood the test of time because they are anchored on a solid base. Your life, also, must sit firmly upon a foundation so strong it can weather the test of time.

At the base of our pyramid is our health. Without health, we have nothing. We cannot be good to anyone if we are sick, exhausted, unstable, emotional, run-down or out of shape. In order to truly *have it all*, we must anchor ourselves in true health, in a way that is meaningful and of a personal definition. Furthermore, alongside health is our ability to stay in faith and self-love. These two additional factors create such a solid foundation that a woman becomes unshakable.

In the next three chapters we will work toward creating a solid foundation in your life. The winds may blow, the earth may shake and the rain may pour down, but with a solid base you can always withstand life's storms.

Health is Personal

"I knew that was really the only purpose of life: to be our self, live our truth, and be the love that we are." —Anita Moorjani, *Au*

Anita Moorjani was diagnosed with cancer in April of 2002. After seeing multiple specialists her prognosis was grim; Moorjani had stage four cancer and was told she would die. In her book, Dying to be Me, she chronicles her journey from health to her initial diagnosis to denial and finally hovering over her body as the doctors worked on her. She made a decision to come back, to return to her body, to share her story, and today she is cancer-free.

Ask anyone who has journeyed back from the edge – the place in which we either choose to die or will ourselves, through God's grace, to live – and they will tell you that health is extremely personal; it is entirely of our own definition. Once health has been lost – for days, months or even years – and reclaimed, its value eclipses diamonds, rubies, gold or the greatest fortunes in the world. When I came back after three years of suffering with MS, I felt, and still feel, that every day is a gift…a gift from God.

Almost every health challenge of the modern age is rooted in self-harm. We are eating too much; we are eating foods that are full of pesticides, herbicides, chemicals, additives, hormones and more. We are leaning on fast food. We are eating foods that are genetically modified. Convenience has become paramount, and that has led us to be in a dire state of health today where obesity claims hundreds of thousands of lives every year and there are more people who are overweight in the world than those who are starving to death.

For some reason we have lost the fundamentals of eating whole foods, exercising daily, getting adequate sleep and drinking plenty of water. As a society we look for the "quick fix." We take diet pills that rev us up. We take sleeping pills to calm us down. Prescription medications now cause more accidental death in America than any other source. In essence, we do more things to challenge our health than we do to support it.

The average woman is using caffeine and alcohol to give her both energy and calm her nerves. Stimulant use is on the rise, with the energy drink industry approaching one trillion dollars globally. We look externally for ways to feel "better" all the while numbing ourselves. This isn't a way to live and the reality is that we may never know how bad we feel until we start feeling good.

Many women equate the number on the scale with their health; the lower the number, the healthier they are. I used to do this myself, only ever allowing any positive emotions toward my body if I "lost weight." The sad part of this was that I would hate myself when I gained weight. It was a constant cycle of love and hate. Years of bulimia and anorexia combined with binge eating destroyed my metabolism. Every time I looked in the mirror, I hated what I saw; to me I was inadequate, a failure and someone who lacked willpower.

Being diagnosed with MS was the best thing that could have happened to me. Instead of gauging health by a number, I shifted to focusing instead on how I felt. When I had energy, my immune system was high and I felt happy, then I felt healthy. Today I do not weigh myself at all. I allow the fit of my clothes to guide me. I eat a plant-based diet combined with protein shakes and plenty of vitamins, minerals, omegas and more. I feel healthier than I ever have in my life and the most important thing is that this journey has taken me to a place of simple surrender, asking myself each and every day to see myself as God sees me.

In 1 Corinthians 6:20, it says, "honor the Lord with your body." Our bodies are the veritable carrier of our soul – the soul that is Divinely created – and it is our responsibility to care for this vessel of Divinity. We are not at war with our body; the body is simply expressing disharmony of the soul. By caring for our health, we re-establish harmony and that brings all other aspects of our life into greater balance.

At the base of the *have it all* life pyramid is health. Health is the foundation that allows us to live into the divine women we were destined to be. With true health we can be better partners, friends, lovers, citizens, humanists and live into all of the other aspects of our lives more fully – more vibrantly. When we are healthy, every part of our life improves. In this chapter we will go step by step, focusing on your health and creating a solid foundation for truly having it all.

Take a moment to meditate on what true health means to you. Imagine a life where you have the energy and stamina to do anything from running a marathon, to keeping up with your children or grandchildren, to climbing Mount Kilimanjaro, to whatever you can possibly fathom. Know that no matter where you are, you can always improve. Anita Moorjani's story illustrates that even if one is lying on a table, hovering above one's body, it is never too late.

You Define Your Age

"Don't let your age be an obstacle. Remember: It's never too late to start. Thus we never get too old to experience something new. Be patient. Your body is a very faithful instrument and will respond to your commands."

— Sister Madonna Buder, *Nun and Athlete*

Sister Madonna Buder is not your average nun. At the age of 23 she entered the convent and dedicated her life to Christ. At the age of 48 she began to run, bike and swim, at the behest of Father John, who said that it would allow her to calm her mind. By age 52 she entered her first triathlon. Today, in her eighties, Sister Madonna has done well over three hundred triathlons, including several Ironman's (a 2.4-mile swim, 112-mile bike and 42-mile run). In the triathlon world she is known as the "Iron Nun."

Many women will lament that they are too old. I have heard women in their early forties speak about how their bodies are aging. Conversely, I have observed many women jealously lament that women can do things simply because they are younger. The truth is that age is what we make of it. The second truth is that just because someone is of a certain age does not necessarily make them more capable of an achievement. There are many younger people who are sick, stricken with diseases such as heart disease, cancer, fibromyalgia, arthritis and multiple sclerosis – diseases that were previously associated with older women.

By taking care of our bodies, fueling our health with whole foods, getting adequate rest, exercising and taking care of ourselves we can truly define our age; in other words we can make of it what we choose. When I was in my early thirties my doctor informed me that I had the blood panel of a ninety-five year old. I felt tired, I ached, I was depressed, I couldn't sleep and I was sure that this is what it felt like to be old. Today, I feel younger than ever – the result of a careful diet, bio-identical hormones (more on that later in this chapter), daily meditation and spending more time listening to my body.

There are many advances in the "youthful aging" movement. By investing in your health now you will most likely not have to invest in illness later. Our bodies are truly miraculous and regenerate every seven years. Even if you have been a smoker, abused your body with drugs and alcohol, consumed foods that contain artificial ingredients or harmed your body, you can come back. Health is absolutely the foundation of our lives and it is imperative that you value your body so that you can truly live into the *have it all woman* you were destined to be.

You are What You Eat—Literally

"If slaughterhouses had glass walls the whole world would be vegetarian."

— Linda McCartney, *Advocate*

Our body is comprised of one hundred trillion cells. These cells rely on ingested nutrients for optimal function. When we consume food, whether whole, organic, processed, or artificial, our body must do its best to break down the food into small particles that can then be used to build cells and cell structures. Inherently, all foods can literally become our body. My question for you is this—what is your body made of?

We are consuming more synthetic, genetically-modified and unnatural food than ever before. On a daily basis we hear about an outbreak of E. coli or some other deadly bacterial strain that can cause symptoms ranging from diarrhea to death. Our farming practices are so industrialized that animal agriculture has become the number-one cause of greenhouse gas emissions in the world.

Our farming practices are also a source of endless atrocities. Our treatment of animals is often cruel at best. Tossing live baby chicks into "shredders," throwing live hogs into boiling water, disemboweling only "partially" dead cattle—the list is endless. In his book, Eating Animals, Jonathon Safran Foer writes, "Perhaps in the back of our minds we already understand, without all the science I've discussed, that something terribly wrong is happening. Our sustenance now comes from misery. We know that if someone offers to show us a film on how our meat is produced, it will be a horror film. We perhaps know more than we care to admit, keeping it down in the dark places of our memory – disavowed. When we eat factory-farmed meat we live, literally, on tortured flesh. Increasingly, that tortured flesh is becoming our own."

In essence, we are truly what we eat. I have personally followed a plant-based diet for years and much of what my children eat comes from plant sources. Clients who have adopted a plant-based approach have experienced improved mood, weight loss, energy gain, improved digestion, better sleep, clearer skin and much more. If not from a purely personal reason, such as improved health, consider the ethical reasons. If you are not sure how your animal products are being farmed—and don't think that just because it reads "organic" or "free-range" that it is—find out.

This is your body, and the only one you have. Everything will become part of your body, it will affect your body and it will ultimately dictate your health. Many of the world's top diseases, including heart disease, cancer, and diabetes, can be minimized by adopting a healthier diet. Ultimately, you must make your own choice; however, I suggest keeping a food log and writing down everything you eat and how you feel throughout the day. After seven days you will begin to see if there is something you are consuming that is potentially causing you not to feel well. If something doesn't make you feel good, stop eating it.

You Have the Power to Heal Your Body

"As your understanding of life continues to grow, you can walk upon this planet safe and secure, always moving forward toward your greater good."

— Louise Hay, *Author*

Louise Hay, best-selling author of Heal Your Life, is herself a cancer survivor. When she was diagnosed with cervical cancer she saw it as an opportunity to reconcile old hurts, including divorce and sexual and physical abuse. Ms. Hay credits her faith in the healing power of God and choosing to release all anger, blame and judgment as the catalysts for the cancer leaving her body. Today, she continues to lecture all over the world as an author and speaker sharing the message that all disease in our bodies is simply "dis-ease."

People have disagreed with Louise Hay and many others who have been able to champion recovery from illness and even death. Those who vehemently argue that it is impossible to treat illness without medication are sadly people who have disharmony in their own bodies. As someone who did not use medication to treat her MS, I truly believe that the body can turn illness on and it can turn illness off.

That being said, it is imperative that we use a healthy lifestyle to be proactive when it comes to our health and our healing. Sleep, meditation and prayer, healthy foods and regular exercise are all enormous contributors to overall well-being. Know that if you are struggling through an illness, or have in the past, then it is never too late to become a champion in your own life. Simply choose to begin with taking care of yourself, and putting your health at the forefront and watch the miracles unfold. The body is indeed miraculous and we do, through the grace of God, have the power to heal ourselves.

In this chapter you might need to embrace the 'D' of dumping the notions you may have acquired that your age or an illness determines how you should live your life. These are stories we tell ourselves – stories that our disempowering to our spirit. The truth is that by letting go of any limiting false beliefs you now step into a place of infinite potential where you can absolutely live into a beautiful healthy body.

Put Your Oxygen Mask on First

"I'm very definitely a woman and I enjoy it." — Marilyn Monroe, *Actress*

Previously, we discussed the power of creating a pyramid for your life, the importance of letting go of guilt and putting your health first. At this point you may be thinking, "I can't put my health first; that would be selfish." You are not alone; many women feel the same way, and I was once of the same mindset, pushing myself to extremes until I became exhausted, depressed, resentful and miserable.

If you have ever traveled on an airplane, you may recall the safety overview. I have been flying for so long that I remember when people were allowed to smoke on airplanes, which I find incredibly funny considering all of the potential dangers. We have, however, come a long way, and today the safety overview is often performed by video, instead of by a person, on what are now smoke-free flights.

In the video, when they get to the part about the oxygen mask, they always instruct parents to put the mask on themselves before they put it on their child. This is done for obvious reasons, because if the parent loses oxygen then there is no one to save the child.

Your health is no different. How do you expect to be of benefit to anyone if you do not put your well-being first? How can you be a good mother, partner, friend, lover, employee, business owner or anything at all if you are not energized and healthy? The simple answer is that you can't.

As women, the decision to put ourselves first is often laden with guilt. How can we put ourselves in front of our children, job, partner, family and friends? In my courses and seminars, I assist women with re-framing the notion of putting themselves first. I teach that it is more selfish to put yourself last, because as the resentment builds everyone and everything else suffers. Yes, you may have to rearrange your schedule or let certain things go in order to get workouts in and take extra time to prepare foods; however, what do you gain by watching extra television or surfing the Net? The answer is not much.

What does it really take to put yourself first? It is simple: it starts by making a decision. Simply make a decision that your day will be better when you take care of your health. At present you may not know what that looks like, and honestly, for each woman, there are variables that contribute to our overall health and well-being. What matters most, at this moment, is that you understand that by choosing to be the healthiest you, you can be, you now open the door of infinite possibilities in your life.

A Starting Point

"To keep the body in good health is a duty. . . otherwise we shall not be able to keep our mind strong and clear." — Buddha

All things must have a beginning. You may be fit and healthy, you may be obese, you may be lying in a hospital bed or somewhere in between. Wherever you are right now is your starting point. There may be a great deal of change required or very little. Regardless of the magnitude, change can be frightening. Change is also necessary, because to go on exactly as you are means to have no difference in the outcome.

Change takes commitment. So many women wish they could continue on the same path and experience a different result. They look to pills, magic diets, certain types of exercise and an entire array of things to achieve what they consider to be optimal health. Your body is a result of what you do consistently; therefore, change will not happen in a day or even a week. Once we find a routine that yields results we must stay with it and not withdraw in fear or look to the next best thing.

Sarah's Story

When our children were ages five and one we moved to a small town. As part of my new, slower-paced routine, I took Avery to school every morning and had an opportunity to socialize with the other mothers. One of the women was Sarah, a very attractive and outgoing gal with great energy who always seemed cheerful and happy. She was a person I truly wanted to get to know better. We passed day after day, though, never really having an opportunity to deeply connect.

Time went by and we moved to a new home further out of the city. By this time, our daughter was going to a new school and it happened that Sarah's children were also going to this school and we were all living on the same street. I decided to make an effort to get to know her better. I asked her if she wanted to go walking after dinner.

Sarah was a breath of fresh air. She was very dedicated to her family, her home and her community. I could see the compassion in her spirit. Sarah was a beautiful woman who constantly laughed in the face of challenge, which was evidenced as she struggled through our walks. At this time, Sarah was about 60 pounds overweight and although she carried it well, I could see that this bothered her.

No matter how we want to help someone or how many answers we think we possess, I have learned to be respectful and allow the person to ask questions.

When someone asks us questions they are opening the door for the answer. The biggest mistake we can make is to push so hard that it affects relationships. I knew Sarah was struggling and I knew that I had some great solutions. However, it took her being ready for me to assist.

One day as we were walking up a particularly steep hill Sarah turned to me in slight frustration and said, "I am sweating and you are not even breathing hard. You are wearing flip flops and I can't even keep up. What is it you do to be so healthy?" At that moment the door was open.

I shared with Sarah about the life pyramid. I shared with her that health is our greatest blessing and that it allows us to be better in every area of our lives. I told her about detoxification, eating properly and putting high-quality nutrition in her body. Then, I said nothing. I allowed her to ask me questions.

She asked many questions. She was curious and cautious at the same time. She told me that she could never run. She told me that she didn't really like to drink water. I let her continue until we got to the true root of the issue. She finally said, "I lost all this weight once and then it came back."

I knew we had found our starting point. I saw that this was where her pain was. Sarah was compensating in her life. She was the person everyone counted on. She was the best friend, the chauffeur, the PTA organizer, the meticulous homeowner and much more. All of this was masking the pain she felt about her health. Additionally, the fear was so great that she would not be able to maintain a healthy body that she didn't even want to try. I witnessed the anger and frustration in her voice.

I asked Sarah how committed she was to her goal weight of 155 pounds. She said, "100%." I then asked her if she would be willing to trust me. She agreed. Now the door was fully open and I stepped through to assist Sarah.

We started with a full-body detoxification and taking a look at her eating habits. In her first week and a half she released 10 pounds, had more energy, was more attentive to her children and absolutely over the moon with the initial results. Sarah was ready for the next step, which was increasing her exercise routine. She began with daily powerwalks and abdominal crunches. She also changed her diet to include vitamins, minerals and daily protein shakes. At mealtimes there were more vegetables, as well as protein and complex carbohydrates. Sarah increased her water intake to twelve cups or more every day. The pounds melted off.

One year later Sarah was 70 pounds lighter and running 3-6 miles/day. She still looks incredible. Her confidence has soared. She and her husband are in the process of starting a business. She is a powerful *Have It All Woman*. All Sarah needed to do was give herself permission to put herself first – to allow herself to get healthy without guilt or fear. We are all capable of transformation and once we have made a decision to get healthy and even attract one or more people who believe in us, we can then set goals to keep ourselves focused, stay motivated, inspired and provide manageable targets to monitor our progress.

What Is Your Destination?

"I wouldn't dream of working on something that didn't make my gut rumble and my heart want to explode." — Kate Winslet, *Actress*

All journeys must have a destination. Your goals are that destination. You must know what you want to achieve with your health. Perhaps you wish to breathe free and clear, maybe it is to have your body free of resistance, or it could be around pain, weight, fatigue, cravings and so much more. The reality is that you must have health goals that are meaningful to you. Be unique.

Always write your goals in the present and create them in the positive. Instead of saying, "I want to lose fifteen pounds," say, "I am in the process of weighing ______." Instead of saying, "I am fighting cancer," say, "My body is in the process of being the picture of health." When we focus on getting rid of something we create resistance and it often comes back.

In Maui there is a stretch of visually stimulating and technical driving called the Road to Hana. The drive is somewhat technical and guidebooks caution that if one is prone to carsickness they should avoid it altogether. I have driven the road and can share from experience that as one twists and turns, both hands on the steering wheel, focusing on the road ahead, there is little opportunity to take in the lush, dense rain forest and breathtaking majesty of the mountains. Oncoming cars, cyclists and hikers all add to the need to be vigilant behind the wheel.

On parts of the drive there are scenic vistas and areas that one call pull over, go for a short hike through a bamboo forest, swim under a waterfall and pause to take a breath. This refreshes the driver, allowing one to return to the road with a new sense of attention on the objective: getting to Hana.

Like this road, heading toward your goal may have twists and turns; it may also have scenic vistas. It is important to relish the small victories along the way and take that time to pause, taking it all in. Having worked for decades with women who want to release weight, for example, I have had many who become frustrated when they reach a plateau. A plateau is much a like a scenic vista; your body is simply taking time to reset itself and establish a new set point weight.

Whether your goal is releasing weight or running a marathon, all large goals come with smaller components. Love yourself enough to savor the journey, reset along the way and celebrate every victory.

Could You Do One Thing Every Day?

"I like to take up something that is challenging. I like to stretch myself."

— Christine Lahti, *Actress*

Now that you have your health goals down, let me ask you – could you do at least one thing every day to move yourself closer to your goals? Could you drink more water? Could you get more rest? Could you clean up your eating? Could you make time for exercise? Remember, without your health you can be of little good to anyone – despite your best intentions – so the time for change is now, no matter how much resistance you may be feeling.

When I am working with people who have specific health goals, I ask for their commitment level on a scale from one to ten with ten being the absolute highest. If their answer is not a ten I know they are not very dedicated to the goal. At this point, we go back and look at the possible fears around achieving their goal. Perhaps they feel more pressure when they are lean, perhaps they feel that no matter what they do they won't achieve it, and lastly, perhaps this goal is for someone else.

My good friend, Lisa, suffered a massive stroke at the young age of thirty. For three years she struggled with life's simple daily tasks. At certain points she even needed her husband to help her use the bathroom. She felt humiliated, embarrassed and hopeless in her life.

After several years of therapy and the unconditional love from her family, Lisa began to heal. She eventually returned to her old self, though she still lived in fear, often struggling to cope. The nightly glass of wine turned into a bottle. Lisa gained so much weight that she didn't recognize herself. She finally reached her tipping point when she realized that if she kept on going the way she was going she might not have another stroke, but it could be a heart attack or something else that would lead to an early death.

Her transformation began simply by deciding to stop drinking. It was one day at a time. The next step was to put better food in her body. She began with a cleanse and then increased her intake of whole foods, protein shakes and vitamins. Once she cleaned up her eating she decided to start exercising – just a few times per week at first and then she gradually increased to the point where she began entering figure competitions. Today she holds her IFBB pro card and her family could not be more proud.

Lisa's story is a wonderful example of how making one change at a time can lead to a complete transformation. As women we often go "all out," only to "burn out." By simply doing one or two things at a time, getting comfortable with those changes, and then adding more, we prevent overwhelm and ease into what will be permanent lifestyle changes.

In the remaining portion of this chapter on health, we will cover the key factors that influence how we look and feel, followed by strategies for getting to your next level of health. I encourage you to read through these and make a decision to adopt one or two new habits and then come back and adopt one or two more.

Remember, your health is the foundation to everything you can achieve in your life. I know that you are destined for greatness and truly can live out the secret desires of your heart. Let's get you healthy so you can truly *have it all.*

Take Responsibility

"The secret of health for both mind and body is not to mourn for the past, nor to worry about the future, but to live the present moment wisely and earnestly." — Buddha

No matter where we are, we must consider it a starting point. The tendency we have as women is to look in the mirror every day and beat ourselves up for the body we do not have. It is easier to look at ourselves with condemnation and complain than to see our beauty. We are all incredible creations of God. Regardless of what you see in the mirror, you can choose to enhance your creation by taking responsibility for your health.

Early in my personal training and nutrition career there was a client who assured me that she ate healthy every day. I would go to her home and train her five times every week, putting her through grueling workouts that left her sweating and breathless. Regardless of the intensity, she was not losing weight. She became fitter as a result of the consistency, but no matter how challenging the workouts became, the scale did not budge.

She asked me to create an eating program for her. I obliged, thinking that she would at this point start to release weight. When nothing happened she began to take her frustrations out on me, telling me that I wasn't putting her through the proper exercises and that the diet was not working. I internalized her frustrations. I tried harder to find answers. I beat myself up for not being good enough to help her lose weight.

After several months of frustration for both of us, I blamed myself for not being good enough. One night I was at a party and overheard a conversation with my client's mechanic. He was sharing a story about how my client needed to have her car detailed every week because of the huge number of chocolate bar wrappers on the floor. I breathed a massive sigh of relief. It wasn't the exercise or my eating program that was to blame for the lack of results; it was the sabotage on behalf of my client.

What my client lacked was personal responsibility. She blamed me, and likely others, for her lack of results. When it comes to our health, we will never progress until we take personal responsibility for our actions and our lives. To be truly healthy is to understand that, ultimately, although it may not feel like it, we are in control.

It is said that many roads lead to the same destination. In terms of health, there are always many methods by which to change our circumstances. These methods, or strategies, may seem so simple – such as drinking more water – that we devalue them. However, studies show that over time, this alone can contribute to fat loss. Inherently, some of the easiest things yield the greatest results.

For years, I operated on about six hours of sleep every night, telling myself that I could function. I knew that conventional wisdom dictated that we required seven hours. Furthermore, I had also studied that the sleep between ten o'clock p.m. and two o'clock a.m. was the most critical to stimulate growth hormone production. Regardless, I continued to go to bed late and wake up early.

After a trip to Bali, I came home and fell into a pattern of going to be by nine o'clock at night and getting up at four thirty in the morning. Not only did I have more production time; I also dropped a stubborn five pounds even though I was eating more. My hormones balanced out, my skin cleared up and I felt greater joy in my life. After this I was "sold" on sleep. That being said, with my travel schedule I do not always get seven and a half hours of sleep, and it does catch up with me. My skin starts to break out, I feel more stress and that pesky five pounds comes back. Sleep didn't seem like such a big deal until I began getting more and my health went to the next level.

Some strategies, conversely, may take more effort or financial investment, such as finding a good integrative physician to assist with hormone balance, getting regular massage, doing a good detox, or taking a meditation class. However, these can all be life-transforming.

I had a girlfriend who had been diagnosed with bipolar disorder, was put on medication and had to stop working for ten years. Sadly, she was also a single mother and times were tough. Fortunately, she had been a good saver through her twenties and somehow managed to get by. Desperate to end the years of living in a fog, my friend decided to detoxify her body and find a new doctor. Today, her hormones are balanced, she is thirty pounds lighter, is working out and has started a business that is bringing in extra income. Her energy and outlook have profoundly changed.

My friend had to invest money and energy to change her outcome and that may be your path as well. Never look at spending money on your health as an expense; think of it as an investment. The more you put in, the more you can give to the world, and for the majority of women, our personal significance is attached to the people and things we contribute to.

A key factor in creating a *have it all* life is to lay a solid foundation in your health. The following are strategies that you can implement to begin to transform your well-being. I suggest you choose one or two areas to focus on at a time. Many women try to change everything at once, and this is often a surefire way to become overwhelmed and ultimately give up. Make a decision that you are going to be the healthiest YOU, you can be, starting today, because not only do you deserve it, everyone else in your life does too.

Strategies for Optimal Health

"Women in particular need to keep an eye on their physical and mental health, because if we're scurrying to and from appointments and errands, we don't have a lot of time to take care of ourselves. We need to do a better job of putting ourselves higher on our own 'to do' list."

— Michelle Obama, *First Lady*

Sleep

Sleep is critical to your health and the deep sleep between ten o'clock p.m. and two o'clock a.m. has been shown to be extremely essential to body repair, regeneration and hormone regulation. During restful sleep your body creates growth hormone which aids in repair and growth of lean tissue. It also assists in stimulating the production of hormones responsible for fat loss. As we age, we secrete less and less growth hormone, so it is imperative that we provide the body with everything it needs, and that includes protein to prevent muscle loss.

Restful sleep can be a challenge in our stressed-out world. People have more demands on their life, including money, work issues, health, family and much more. It is expensive to make a living, let alone live a life. Sleep is often the first thing to suffer as people lie awake at night searching for answers to their problems.

Lack of sleep truly ages us. When we do not get enough, we are not able to function, we become accident-prone, temperamental, and our immune system suffers. Growth hormone, which is topped up while we sleep, tends to decrease when we do not get a minimum of 7 - 8 hours of solid rest. When growth hormone levels go down, so do other hormones, such as those that are required to release stubborn body fat.

When we get enough sleep, our skin glows, we feel energized and focused. We have energy for work, play and exercise. We also tend to be less hungry because when people are tired they crave carbohydrates to stay awake. The body begins to ease down at around two o'clock in the afternoon. In many countries they rest at this time. In North America, Australia, parts of Europe and Asia, however, we are all reaching for lattes, tea and cookies to keep us going.

I have had many clients who struggled with getting adequate sleep. It takes time to change a sleep pattern but the results are absolutely worth it in terms of looking and feeling better. Here are 10 tips that have been found to be effective:

1. Keep a sleep log. Record your hours of sleep and how you feel the next day.
2. Avoid all caffeine drinks after lunchtime. This includes diet and regular sodas, coffee and tea.
3. Drink a protein shake, preferably one that is high in tryptophan, a naturally occurring amino acid that promotes calm and relaxation. Supplemental 5HTP can be helpful. Ask your health practitioner to advise.

4. Calcium helps with a more restful sleep. I suggest powdered or liquid calcium, which has a higher absorption rate. Make sure your calcium also has vitamin D and magnesium.
5. Limit fluids, with the exception of your shake, which you can take at least 2 hours before bedtime. This will assist you in not having to get up and use the bathroom.
6. Alcohol can also lead to restlessness during sleep so avoid it until you change your sleep cycle.
7. Begin your wind down for sleep one hour prior to bedtime. I suggest reading something positive or listening to a meditation audio.
8. Keep a notebook and pen beside your bed. One reason people have a hard time getting to sleep is because their minds are racing. If you wake up because you suddenly remember something—this happens to me—then you can write it down and release the worry that you will forget.
9. Start your bedtime routine at the same time every night. Use deep breathing from your lower abdomen to relax your body.
10. Avoid television, the internet and articles that contain violence. Sleep research has found that these images go into your subconscious and will disrupt sleep. Also eliminate all screens from your bedroom.

Exercise

Exercise is perhaps the greatest blessing you can give your body. Exercise relieves stress and tension, burns calories, increases metabolism and assists the lymphatic system in releasing waste.

Exercise is broken down into two main forms: cardiovascular and resistance training

Cardiovascular exercise increases your heart rate and burns more calories than resistance exercise; however, resistance training is also important because it creates muscle which helps us metabolize more calories at rest. Walking, running, swimming, aerobics, dancing and cycling are just a few examples of cardiovascular workouts.

In the early Twentieth century and prior to that, people had active work and tended to walk more. With the advent of the industrial era, as well as increased technology, people decreased the amount of cardiovascular exercise they got in their day-to-day lives.

Today, many people have sedentary jobs, and schools are cutting down on physical education. It is no wonder that waistlines are increasing.

To release body fat you need a minimum of 40 minutes every day of cardiovascular exercise. 20 minutes will maintain fitness. Exercising 3 times per week will also not yield significant gains. Cardiovascular exercise should be done 5-6 times per week and at varied intensities.

For example, one day you may do an easy jog. On another day you may take a boxing class. You can vary your activities; all the heart knows is that it is pumping more blood. You will burn more calories from fat during cardiovascular workouts than during resistance training, but it is the muscle created from resistance exercise that burns more fat at rest. In other words, you need both types of exercise.

Resistance training involves using free weights, machine, bands or body weight exercises such as yoga and Pilates. Resistance training can also strengthen your bones. Women, especially, should do resistance training once they reach thirty to assist the body in preserving bone density.

I suggest you consult a certified personal trainer to assist you in creating a proper resistance workout. Also, go to your local health club or get a DVD of a Pilates or yoga class. These are great ways to tone and shape muscles.

Exercise plays a major role in your body and there is supporting evidence that people who exercise have less body fat than those who do not. For your best body ever, I suggest doing 40 minutes or more of exercise 5-6 days/week. Always consult your physician before commencing an exercise program.

As women, life happens. Our days are filled with demands. We may get a call from the school letting us know we need to pick a child up or we may realize that there is not enough in the house to make dinner and the next day's lunches and so our workout time becomes sabotaged. Get your workout done in the morning, even if it means going to bed earlier and rising an hour before everyone else. You will feel better, you will be happier, and most of all, you are setting yourself up for a solid foundation to the day.

Eat Smaller Portions and Eat More Frequently

In North America and all over the world people are eating too much. Portion sizes have grown over the last few decades due to easier access to food and more efficient transportation methods. Calorie consumption has increased decade after decade since the 1970's. It is becoming more common to see all-you-can-eat buffets and unlimited refills on soda. The sad result is that the world is killing itself one mouthful at a time.

The major challenge is that, as humans we are now consuming more calories than ever before and getting less exercise than generations past. Research conducted at University of North Carolina analyzed data from surveys done in the seventies, eighties, nineties and the first decade of two thousand, looking at calorie consumption in a twenty-four hour period. Their findings were:

1970's — 1803 calories/day

Today — 2374 calories/day

There are 3500 calories in one pound of fat. Basically, an extra five hundred calories per day will yield an extra pound of body fat every week. Once fat cells are created by the body they can never be destroyed; they can only be shrunk.

The best way to nourish the body is to consume smaller meals throughout the day. The human body can only properly digest about 600 calories in one sitting. Anything beyond this can easily be converted to fat. Body builders, fitness and figure athletes are the masters of proper portion size. They will alternate protein shakes and small meals like tuna, a baked potato and steamed broccoli.

Eating 200-600 calories every 3 hours is ideal. If you are trying to gain mass, these 600-calorie meals would be best. If you are trying to lose fat, then alternate 200-calorie meals with 400- to 600-calorie meals.

A rule of thumb I have recommended for years is that you put vegetables on your plate first and let them take up most of the room, protein second and starches last. This will give you the correct ratio.

A fist size of meat, chicken, tempeh or fish is about all your body is able to digest. There are 7 grams of protein in every ounce of meat or fish. Therefore 4-5 ounces would contain 28-35 grams. People truly overeat protein and carbohydrates.

Thick sauces, salad dressings and gravies tend to be loaded with calories. Keep these to a minimum. One tablespoon of regular salad dressing has about 100 calories so be cautious even when eating healthy foods.

Another tip for portion control is not to let yourself get too hungry. Before going to a party where there will be lots of food, have a protein shake or half of a protein bar. My mentor also suggested having protein-rich foods, such as shrimp, at parties, which are low in calories as well.

At home, wait 20 minutes before going for second helpings. The body takes 20 minutes to register fullness. People often head back for seconds before they feel truly full. In fact, your stomach is only about the size of your fist, so be cautious when it comes to filling your plate for a second time.

Sparkling water can also trick the body into thinking it is full. Keep sparkling mineral water on hand. Alcoholic beverages can pile on the pounds due to high calories. Additionally, when you consume alcohol, you are more likely to overeat.

Food Choices

On the subject of creating meals, we all have different likes and dislikes. Our food choices are a reflection of time, cost, convenience and taste. In this era when people are busier than ever before, and many people are working longer hours, it is no wonder we are a so called fast food nation.

In my travels I have seen popular fast food outlets in Guatemala, and a preponderance of fast food in Asia and Europe. It is not just a North American phenomenon. Oddly enough, many of these countries are now reporting higher obesity rates as the fast food giants move in. It doesn't take much common sense to figure out that one double hamburger has more calories than a bowl of soup with noodles, vegetables and shrimp.

As people get fatter, busier and more stressed they tend to reach for convenience foods. I travel just as much as the next person but I learned long ago from my Girl Guide leader, Mrs. McDougall, to always be prepared. I travel with protein bars, a package of protein shakes, snack wafers, vitamins and antioxidants.

As I am dashing through airports I will pick up a greens drink and some raw almonds or trail mix. Maintaining my energy is important. A large herbal tea also does the trick. Green tea is rich in antioxidants and has some powerful nutrients that assist the body in releasing fat.

It is important for me to have strong mental focus and high energy. My days can be really long, with 5 kids, writing, speaking, investing and building businesses. I must fuel my body with the very best nutrition. We keep healthy foods in the house so that if/when we do get really hungry we won't be reaching for junk.

It has been said that what goes in must come out and this is absolutely true for your food choices. If you are eating lots of sugar, it will come out in mood highs and lows and also put you at risk for diabetes, obesity and more.

If you are eating a lot of saturated fats like those found in beef, pork and butter, then you are at risk for heart disease, stroke, and even cancer.

Your mother was right when she told you to eat your fruits and vegetables. The famous Framingham Study found that by simply eating 5-7 servings of fresh fruits and vegetables every day, one can reduce the risk of cancer by 70%. If you are challenged in getting fresh fruits and vegetables consistently then I suggest getting a greens supplement.

Eat a Hormone Healthy Diet

Dr. Natasha Turner, author of The Hormone Diet, suggests that women eat quality foods in order to keep hormones in balance. She suggests consuming healthy fats such as avocadoes, olives and raw nuts at each main meal and choosing produce that is organic. Additionally, for animal products, Dr. Turner advises we choose wild, organic and hormone-free.

Much of the undoing of our hormone health is linked to our food and how it is farmed and raised. Many women have hormones that are out of balance, causing mood swings, anxiety, acne, weight gain, depression and more. Much of this can be eliminated by eating foods that have not been treated with steroids and hormones.

Supplementation

Supplementation simply means to add into the diet the nutrients that are not coming from food. For many people, adding vitamins, minerals, protein, probiotics, enzymes and other nutrients helps them create and maintain a healthier body. As soils become depleted and their produce increasingly deficient in nutrients, we as consumers end up short-changed in terms of what we need to sustain us on a daily basis.

When an individual requires supplementation and isn't getting it, they can have a variety of issues, including weight gain, lowered immune system, poor skin and nails, lack of mental acuity, irritability and an entire host of diseases. Hypothyroidism has been linked to iodine deficiency, diabetes to a lack of chromium in the soil, and recent studies have linked multiple sclerosis to vitamin D deficiency.

Nutritionally-linked disease states are complex and there are many theories. The best thing you can do for yourself is to work with a practitioner, such as a naturopathic doctor or physician, who also works with natural products and who can create a sound eating program which may include supplements.

Supplementation is as old as time. Thousands of years ago people took tonics to boost everything from fertility to virility. In many cultures today it is not uncommon to boil herbs and create teas and tonics to assist in better health.

In North America supplementation is a growing industry, with more people on a quest for excellent health. Even the skin care industry is getting on board with more and more beauty companies coming out with orally administered vitamins to create healthier skin. I was in Boston recently at an upscale cosmetics store, and yes, even found a section with a number of these vitamins.

Traditional science is coming around to the notion of supplementation. Many physicians agree that women generally need to supplement with vitamins, calcium and often iron (for women of childbearing age) at the very minimum. Doctors frequently put pregnant women on a prenatal vitamin. Why should vitamins only be important when you are pregnant? What about year-round health?

For the purpose of this book I will do a brief overview of some of the more popular supplements and, at the very least, those which may be of interest to you.

Antioxidants

Many studies also illustrate the need for antioxidant supplementation. Antioxidants are vital in protecting the body from free-radical damage. Free radicals are cell scavengers and can cause cell mutation. This cell mutation can lead to disease and premature aging. This is why the skin care giants all use antioxidants in their formulations.

Today there are many excellent antioxidant formulations. You really do not need to supplement them all individually. Vitamins A, C, and E are the major antioxidants, but bilberry, L-glutamine, grape seed extract, milk thistle, cysteine, lutein and many others also have antioxidant properties. Find a formulation that is right for you and work with your practitioner, especially if you are on medication.

Multi-Vitamins

Multi-vitamins have truly evolved. There are now formulations for every stage of your life. Some have additional digestive enzymes to assist in absorption. Others are encapsulated in a vegetarian capsule for ease of digestion.

Multi-vitamins often include vitamin B, which is useful in dealing with stress, nerve function, and even mood. Some multi-vitamins include iron, which is somewhat controversial as it has been shown to prevent the absorption of other nutrients.

Choose a multi-vitamin that is not covered in dye. Find something that also breaks down in vinegar within 30 minutes. This will tell you whether or not it is really breaking down in your system.

Essential Fatty Acids

Essential Fatty Acids, or E.F.A.'s for short, have had recent acclaim in their benefits to overall health. E.F.A.'s have been linked to prevention and even anti-aging. Essential Fatty Acids cannot be manufactured in the body and therefore must be consumed from food sources or through supplementation.

Omega-3's and -6's are essential for hormone balance, heart health, brain function, healthy skin, nails, nerve conduction and for "treating" conditions such as candidiasis, eczema and psoriasis. They are found in fish and fish oils, nuts, seeds and certain vegetable oils. Be wary of low-cost omega supplements, as these may contain mercury, which is extremely harmful to the body.

Calcium

Calcium is frequently recommended as a supplement for women as we tend to lose bone density with increasing age. It is also essential for nerve conduction, bone health and has even been linked to fat loss. One study found that women who supplemented with calcium lost more body fat than those who didn't. If you are lactose intolerant you may need to consider supplemental calcium. I use a powdered form for fast absorption.

Supplemental Protein

Protein supplementation is essential for people who, like myself, do not eat meat. These supplements have come a long way. There are now organic protein powder from sources such as hemp, rice, organic whey and more. Protein is critical to muscle growth and repair. It is also a natural appetite suppressant.

Additional Resources

Supplementation can be a key difference in your health. Our bodies require different nutrients based on such things as age, gender, overall health, activity level, climate and stress. When your body gets what it needs, you can look, feel and operate at your best level ever.

For a greater understanding of nutrients, I have two books to suggest. The first is by my great friend Dr. Tony O'Donnell. It is called Miracle Super Foods that Heal. Dr. O'Donnell has been on network television and is a sought-after speaker and product formulator.

The second book is Prescription of Nutritional Healing, by Phyllis Balch. It is updated very frequently. It contains a list of herbs, vitamins, minerals, and macro- and micronutrients. It also has a list of ailments and the nutrients that most alleviate specific conditions.

Build a Support Network of Practitioners and Friends

The Gallup Group found that people who embark on a transformation program with two other people are over sixty percent more likely to be successful. Having others who have similar goals is motivating and can help us stay focused.

Many popular weight-loss programs rely on the support network principle. Personal training is also at a record high because the personal trainer is additional support. Group exercise programs such as water aerobics, dance classes, tai chi, yoga, kick boxing, walking and running clubs also lend support.

Having spent many years in the health and fitness industry, I found that when women felt supported in their goals it created a clearing for their success. If you are not feeling entirely supported at home then get involved with a group, join a class or enroll a friend who can become your exercise and healthy living partner.

In addition to emotional support it is essential to build a team of practitioners. The human body is extremely complex, and for women, even more so. Between giving birth, hormone cycling, stress and a myriad of other life experiences we require a team of people who can work with the intricacies of our bodies.

All women require a general practitioner and some, myself included, have an integrative physician who also specializes in hormones. There is much more to our health than our cholesterol, blood pressure and thyroid levels. An integrative medical professional will also monitor other hormones such as estrogen, progesterone, testosterone and cortisol to maintain homeostasis. Many women have released perceived health challenges – including adult acne, premature hair loss, muscle aches, fatigue, depression, migraines and more – by balancing their hormones through supplementation and natural, bio-identical hormones.

In addition to our primary physician, who will also give us an annual pap smear (believe me – no one enjoys it but it is necessary), we may also choose to have a chiropractor, acupuncturist, registered massage therapist, naturopath, homeopath and others. The most important thing is to find a practitioner who is professional, with whom you have a good working relationship, and whom you can trust. If you feel at all uncomfortable understand that you always have options.

Have Your Breasts Checked Annually

Although the American Cancer Society advocates mammograms for women after the age of forty, they also support BSE or Breast Self Exams that are coached by a physician. Early detection is one of the most critical factors in surviving breast cancer. Not all lumps are cancer; some are fibroids and can be benign. The website www.cancer.org has a wonderful step-by-step diagram on BSE and carefully outlines the different forms of breast exams, from MRI's to mammograms. Always work with your practitioner and book an appointment immediately if you find a lump, have tenderness or swelling unrelated to menses, or severe pain.

I have several girlfriends who have had breast cancer and all survived due to early detection. As women we are, of course, extremely sensitive when it comes to discussing our breasts, and for some women who have been abused or experienced ridicule due to either having large or small breasts, avoidance is common when it comes to breast exams. My message to everyone is to book your exam annually and regularly do a BSE. It could save your life.

Find Alternatives to Medication if Possible

Some medications may make it more challenging to release body fat, stay lean and energized enough to want to create sustainable change. Never go off your medications unless supervised by your doctor; however, if you feel that your medication may be sabotaging your success then consult with your physician to explore alternatives.

For years I suffered with asthma and was prescribed a steroid to treat the condition. I immediately gained over thirty pounds. Although I could breathe, I felt that my body was out of control. For me, going off gluten and dairy allowed me to come off of the steroid and my body leaned out fairly quickly.

Medications were not initially designed to be "for life," though that has become common practice. I highly recommend finding a physician who can work with you to reduce a dependency on pharmaceuticals. Often, by achieving a healthy weight and eating a healthy diet, many medications can be eliminated.

A physician friend once told me that she felt if people would lose thirty pounds they could cut their intake of medication by thirty percent. Many medications are tied to excess weight. As weight reaches healthy levels, blood pressure, blood glucose balance and mood often come into homeostasis. Work with your doctor to devise a plan to regulate your body and reduce dependency on pharmaceuticals whenever possible. Again, never take yourself off of a medication without supervision of your physician.

Work With Your Genetic Blueprint

The truth is that being lean is easier for people who come from families where both the maternal and paternal sides are lean. If one parent is obese there is a 25% chance that the child will be obese. If two parents are obese there is a 50% chance the child will be obese. The jury is still out as to which aspect has a greater role – genetics or environment.

Generational obesity often coincides with lifestyle choices. Obesity was almost nonexistent at the turn of the 20th century. Today almost 30% of North Americans are considered obese. Obesity increases the risk of heart disease, stroke, diabetes and cancer. It also has many non-life threatening effects, such as arthritis and other joint pain.

Being overweight or obese is serious. No one says you have to be thin, but if you want to live a long, fulfilling life you must be healthy. Over time three main body types have emerged in humans, ectomorph, or naturally thin; mesomorph, which is balanced proportionately and would include the majority of athletes; and lastly, endomorph, or naturally heavy.

Basically, if your mother, grandmother and all of your aunts have big hips then chances are you are genetically predisposed to this. Guess what? It just means that you will have to work a little harder and target-train this area with exercise. Body types are changeable. In Sarah's story we saw how a woman who had become obese and had never been smaller than a size ten as an adult, became a size four. It is always possible to reshape your body.

In my family, we are Chinese on one side and Anglo-Saxon on the other. On my dad's side they are slim, trim and big eaters. My husband marvels at "how such small people can eat so much." On my mom's side the women are a little heavier in the thigh and hip area.

For me, I look like my dad's side on top and mom's side on the bottom. Because I was obese as a child I also have to work harder to maintain a lean physique. Growing up was tough because all of my cousins were so slender, and I was a woman's size fourteen at the age of ten. I often cried because I felt so betrayed that I didn't get a tiny body like the other girls in our family.

I was often teased and ridiculed. When I learned to control my portions, eat for health and not to suppress emotions, my body shifted. When I began to cleanse on a regular basis and eat more raw foods my body became leaner and my mind more focused. Today, I am lean and healthy. I still have the same genetics, but I have compensated with diet and exercise.

Working within your genetic blueprint means that you will not follow a "one size fits all" exercise program. For example, women who are generally mesomorphic or endomorphic will often bulk up faster if they consistently life heavier weights. Women who are ectomorphic tend to have a greater risk of osteoporosis and can benefit from lifting heavier weights without the risk of gaining bulk. Find a program that works for your body; this will give you the greatest results and the utmost satisfaction.

Focus on Wellness and Not Illness

Sometimes our bodies get sick. Sometimes this sickness can affect how we look and feel. Illness can affect us in a variety of ways, from a few days in bed with the flu to months of recovery from major surgery or the diagnosis of a disease.

When we do not feel well, emotionally or physically, we often end up eating comfort foods that can result in a loss in muscle and a gain in fat. Sickness can eliminate our resolve, especially if we have chosen to have a victim mentality. Being sick, however, is the worst time to eat foods that do not support the overall health of your body because these types of foods are often the very ones that can further lower the immune system, decrease our energy, and prolong recovery.

If you have been diagnosed or are recovering from an illness, work with a team to reclaim your health. There are so many wonderful complementary therapies that mesh nicely with Western medicine. Getting back on your feet quickly may require a team of people, especially if your illness is complex.

Many women fall into a trap of defining themselves by their disease. They talk about it, they complain about it, and they use it as an excuse for playing small. You are not your disease. You are you – a Divinely created magnificent being whose body happened to turn on a disease and can absolutely turn it off.

In coming back from my MS diagnosis I have worked with acupuncturists, homeopathic doctors, chiropractors, massage therapists, Western doctors, and done cranial sacral work. You may be thinking that the cost of so many treatments is exorbitant, though in comparison with not being able to work, function as a mother and a wife and live my life it is a small price to pay. I also chose not to attend support groups or talk about having MS. I wasn't living in denial; however, I was in no way going to let MS define me as a person.

The biggest thing you can do to assist recovery is work on your attitude. Focus on your recovery and not on your illness. Turn your mindset to the things that bring you joy. Life is too short to let something like disease get you down. There are stories of people who overcome their situation and go on to become healthier than they were before and if you have been diagnosed with an illness then know that you have, within you, the power to absolutely change your circumstances. It begins with making a decision that all things are possible with the right mindset.

If you have been diagnosed with a disease, I recommend reading Louise Hay's You Can Heal Your Life. As we discussed previously, all disease is linked to emotional resistance in the body. By releasing the resistance, you can release the disease.

Deal with Stress in Healthy Ways

Stress will wreak havoc on your body. Stress affects various hormones and neurochemicals in your brain, one of which is cortisol. When cortisol is high we crave sugar, we have difficulty focusing, often it's a challenge having a restful sleep, and yes, there's a tendency to gain weight.

Highly stressed people often have difficulty digesting their food properly and this can lead to other health challenges. Did you know that the majority of heart attacks occur on Sunday night, right before the start of the work week? Stress can affect many areas of your health.

When your body is under a lot of stress it will use more water and even retain water. Additionally, you will use up more minerals as your body requires them to deal with the stress. Stress can also compromise your immune system.

I have had clients who were so stressed that no matter what they did, they could not lose weight. If this is resonating for you then it is imperative you do something about it.

Here are some helpful tips to assist you in releasing stress:

- Get adequate rest. A restful sleep provides a much more positive outlook on a situation.
- Drink plenty of water. Water is key to flushing out excess toxins and even stress hormones from your body.
- Take adaptogens (a group of plants often found in stress formulations) and B-vitamins to help your body to deal with stress.

- Supplement with calcium and Vitamin D3. Both help your body to deal with stress.
- Take a class such as yoga, meditation or Tai Chi. As an aside, I have seen highly stressed people gain weight when they exercise intensely and lose it when they choose gentler options.
- Avoid watching violent television and the news. When we have stress we are prone to elevate our stress by observing situations that are intense.
- Keep a journal to log how you are feeling.
- Seek some form of counseling to deal with the underlying issues.
- Get help with your finances if your stress is due to money problems.
- Take time every week to do something fun and unplug from your technology.

Some of the least stressed people I know work smarter and not harder. They take time every week for some play. Chris and I make sure that every week we have one date night and also family movie night. I don't do business on Sunday, which allows us to play and have fun together as a family. This also gives me time to unplug, refocus on what truly matters and recharge.

Create something in your life that gives you balance and some peace. Life is too short to be in a constant state of worry. I heard something absolutely brilliant once on a television show. The crew was making over the home of a family where the father had died. The host asked if there was something extremely special they could remember about their dad, something he was known for. The children said that their dad had a personal saying: "There are many things to think about, but nothing to worry about." I love this. I think it applies to us all.

Age Truly is Just a Number

After the age of 25 we can lose ¼ to ½ pound of muscle per year. Without proper resistance training and diet, our metabolism can begin to slow down. I have heard people complain many times that they cannot eat in their 40's and 50's what they could in their 20's and it is absolutely true. With increased exercise and boosting your protein intake, you can slow down the gradual age-induced loss of muscle.

Age does not have to be an excuse for anything. One exceptional *have it all woman* I knew didn't start weight training until she was 79. One of my mentors didn't become successful until he was in his seventies. You are as old as you think you are.

Maya Angelou, the American author and poet, says, "There is no agony like bearing an untold story inside of you." No matter what age you are, it is never too early or too late to take control of your health. Start today, don't look back and forever be grateful that you made the commitment to yourself.

Calorie Cycling

Years ago I was blessed to study the work of Tudor Bomba and his team at the University of Toronto. Their research was focused on different training modalities and sports nutrition. They were looking at ways for people to get definition without stimulants or drugs. The studies focused mainly on bodybuilders.

Prior to looking at these studies I also came across some articles touting the benefits of calorie cycling: varying your caloric intake every day, generally in a three-day cycle. This tricks your body into increasing basal metabolic rate so you burn more calories at rest. By simply varying your input, you can fire up your metabolism, allowing you to essentially eat more and weigh less.

When I worked with people who had suffered from eating disorders, I found that they would constantly lower their overall caloric consumption to lose weight. Unfortunately, this practice also slows down the metabolism so even though the calories consumed are lower, the person must continue to decrease the calories even more in order to lose weight. This is extremely dangerous, even in a society where the majority of people overeat.

People who consistently overeat will gain weight. The person who eats an extra 600 calories per day, or the calories equivalent to one large bagel with peanut butter and a banana, could gain one pound per week [illegible] pounds per year. If someone is burning a great deal of calories through exe[illegible]e this may not apply.

They can still use the principles of calorie cycling to be leaner and faster. The truth is whether you eat too much or you eat too little, eventually your body is going to compensate and adapt.

When I first started cycling my own calories, and those of my clients, I started to see impressive results with a decrease in overall body fat, despite having a cheat day every week where we ate whatever we wanted. The cheat day is critical to the program. You must take one day and eat whatever you desire. This will increase your metabolism and allow you both the freedom and peace of mind with your eating.

For calorie cycling it is also critical to journal and keep track of your progress. You will want to use a planner to assist you. Calorie cycling is easy to do, though it will take some getting used to. In these simple-to-follow guidelines you will have a lower-calorie day followed by a medium-calorie day and then a higher-calorie day. You will then follow the pattern again.

On your lower-calorie day you can cut out starches with your evening meal. On the medium-calorie day you can have a smaller portion of starch, such as a ¼ cup of brown rice. On your high-calorie day you can have a small baked potato with dinner. Remember, the potato is not the issue. It is what you put on the potato that counts.

Make sure your meals are lower in saturated fats, such as the fat coming from animals. Healthy fats, such as organic coconut oil, avocadoes, and raw almonds, have been shown to stimulate fat loss, so do include these in your regular diet. Watch sodium intake, as prepared and frozen meals tend to be high in sodium. Have fresh organic fruits and vegetables as often as possible and choose lean cuts of protein such as tempeh, organic eggs, chicken, fish, turkey and game meats. For vegetarians egg whites and protein powders are useful. If you are a vegan find a good-quality vegan protein powder and choose from a variety of beans, legumes, nuts and seeds.

Give Your Body a Rest Once Per Week

Following the calorie cycling formula means that we have two lower calorie days per week. Ideally, you will give your body a rest from exercise on one of these days. Exercising and training seven days per week is very hard on the body.

Additionally, give your body a rest from packaged and prepared foods. I like Harley Pasternak's Five Factor Diet, as his meals include five natural foods and are prepared in five minutes. On your lower-calorie day choose foods that are easier to digest, like steamed vegetables, brown rice, egg whites and oatmeal. Always drink plenty of water on these days.

On a personal note, I cleanse one day per week. On this day I consume a liquid cleansing formula, raw vegetables, fruits and raw almonds. I avoid coffee and tea. I always feel refreshed and energized. This gives my body a break, releases impurities and assists in helping me stay lean.

Frequency of Meals

Many people go for long stretches of time between meals. I have known people who skipped breakfast and eat only at lunch and beyond. I even had one client, the CEO of a company, who ate nothing all day but a muffin and a coffee and then stuffed his face after eight o'clock at night. He was 50 pounds overweight!

The simple truth is that you need to be putting something in your body every 2 ½ to 3 hours. You wouldn't try to start a fire by burning a big log. You need kindling and various smaller things to get it burning. The same thing is true about your metabolism. You want to be constantly fuelling it.

I have helped many people get their bodies into fat-burning mode. It doesn't happen overnight. Some people may feel more energized and revved up within a week or two of changing their eating. For others it may take months.

I was working with a doctor who had ruined his metabolism by eating only protein and no carbohydrates. Initially he lost weight with that program, but after several months he complained of headaches, nausea, constipation and lack of energy. After starting a program that worked with calorie cycling and periodic rest, he soon found himself more energized and losing body fat with ease.

I had another client – a professional hockey player whom everyone thought was past his prime. I changed his fitness program and had him eat three meals and two protein shakes every other day and two meals and two shakes on alternate days. He lost body fat, gained muscle and went on to play another three years in the NHL.

The majority of people feel rotten because their diet is rotten. What goes in must come out. If you put junk in, you will get junk out. If you put healthy, whole-food nutrition in, you feel better. To be a true *have it all woman*, make sure you fuel your body every 2 ½ to 3 ½ hours. Watch what happens to your energy, vitality and waistline.

Plan Your Meals in Advance

Have you ever gone to the grocery store unsure of what you would make for dinner only to forget something or come back with more than you need? Have you ever had to make more than two trips to the store per week? Most women go to the grocery store hungry and unprepared, which wastes valuable time and money.

A great tip is to sit down on Sunday night and plan the week's meals in advance. Write out what you will make and what you require from the store. This will save you trips and save you money.

I had a client once who loved to cook and she was very good at it. Night after night she made gourmet meals for her family, often starting at one in the afternoon. Unfortunately she also had a business and between all of the cooking and the multiple trips to the store (she was there every day), she was wasting a lot of time. By simply planning her meals in advance, we calculated that she saved over two and a half hours per week, which she ended up using on her business.

We all have one thing in common and that is time. When we can be more efficient with our meals it allows us to do the things we love and those things that will move us forward.

Always Be Prepared

Because we travel so often it is imperative that we be prepared. My husband is a true hypoglycemic so I always have meal-replacement bars with me when we travel on airplanes. I often pick up raw vegetables and nuts as I am running through the airport. The worst thing that can happen to you when you are embarking on a lifestyle change is to allow yourself to get too hungry.

I always leave the house with a big bottle of water and snacks. Hunger can sometimes be misconstrued for thirst, so when I feel hungry I drink some water first to see if I am truly looking for food. When you are out doing errands, or at work and living your life, bring easy-to-consume foods with you. Some raw almonds, meal-replacement bars, fresh fruit and raw vegetables will get you through.

Every meal you eat, whether it is on the go or at home, must consist of foods in as natural a form as possible. Natural foods return our body to a natural state. This means choosing whole grains, organic vegetables, fruits, game meats, whole eggs, fish, turkey, chicken, lentils and legumes. Essentially, if you do not know what is on the label or if the food is sweetened, colored or flavored artificially, then it is absolutely going to negatively affect your body.

Your body is a miracle and by shifting to a high-quality diet, your body will soon shift to a new level of health.

Drink Your Water

To achieve the best health possible you will want to drink one half to one ounce per pound of your desired body weight. For example, if your desired body weight is 150 pounds then you would consume 75 to 150 ounces of water per day. The more active you are the higher up the scale you go. Please note that it may take time to build up your water intake and that with increased consumption, you will experience greater fullness and satisfaction. Strangely enough, many people who overeat are actually dehydrated.

Water helps your body deal with stress and keeps your skin looking beautiful. Studies have shown that a well-hydrated body releases not only body fat with greater ease but also allows for more effective flushing of metabolic waste.

For those who have difficulty drinking water, decaffeinated herbal teas could be considered a substitute. Add fresh lemon or a slice of orange to change the flavor of the water. Like any habit, drinking adequate water takes time; however, once your body is consistently hydrated you will not want it any other way.

Keep an Exercise and Eating Journal

As we previously mentioned, those who journal their eating and exercise habits tend to have greater success. Additionally, how will you know what is working and what is not if you are not journaling? Your life and your health should not be random stabs in the dark.

Create your own journal to log what you eat, drink, any exercise you do and how you feel. You will begin to notice patterns. These patterns will assist you in understanding when you are more vulnerable to cravings and overeating. Start your journal today.

Take Care of Your Skin

We have our skin for life. As we age, our skin loses collagen and that causes wrinkles and sagging. Sun damage also ages us and can be a precursor to skin cancer. With pollution, lack of sound nutrition, and other challenges, it is imperative to take care of your skin.

The skin we have in our forties, fifties, sixties and beyond is a reflection of how we care for our skin in our twenties and thirties. Our basic skin care regime should include a gentle cleanser, toner, antioxidant serum, day cream with SPF 30, and a night cream.

Baby Boomers are the largest consumers of skin care products. They want to live freely and age slowly. To live a life of inner beauty is the highest quest. Beautiful skin isn't so bad either, so take care of yours.

Regardless of your budget, there are affordable options for healthy skin care. If you can afford it, I recommend getting a facial every quarter. A facial is an excellent investment in your long-term skin care and not just a luxury. The *have it all woman* can attract the abundance where the cost of skin care and facials do not pose a financial burden.

Lifestyle

Lifestyle is what we do on a consistent basis. It is how we eat, how we rest, how we play and how we work. Lifestyle will define and have the greatest impact on our bodies.

Are you always working? Are you running from one thing to the next? Is your mind constantly going? Do you rush through meals or forget special occasions? Are you consumed with one area of your life? Do you make time for play and rest? I can tell you one thing for sure: many people are out of balance in their life because they are guilty of some if not all of these lifestyle choices.

Have you ever seen someone who operates with ease? They are calm, peaceful, happy, energized and lean? Chances are they have figured out this lifestyle thing and got it down to a science.

In our family our lifestyle includes daily exercise, playing with our kids, working from home, taking one day of rest, connecting as a family, healthy eating and honoring our bodies.

We have just gone over many factors which affect your physical body. Whatever place you are in right now, have hope. Remember that people achieve amazing things all of the time. Right now you are in the right place at the right time and I want to congratulate you for making it this far.

Master Your Thoughts

At some point you will need to focus on the actions, and the results will take care of themselves. In our courses we teach people how to eat for pleasure and nutrition as opposed to eating for pain. We also teach a principle that defines "feeding the hole," a concept that stresses the importance of conscious eating.

In our quest for the best body we can achieve, it is critical that we do not compare ourselves to others. We can only control our own thoughts, actions, beliefs and outcomes. How others look is of little or no concern. Our focus must remain on our quest to be the best we can be.

How we view our health will be in direct relation to what manifests. If our attitude is poor, our health will likely be poor. To be the master of our thoughts and not indulge in self-pity is a lifelong quest and one which is extremely worthwhile. Know that you can do whatever you dream as long as you focus in and have faith that it will come to you.

It is natural to want to be somewhere else with your health. I struggled for years because I compared myself to others. When I saw a woman who was thin, I envied her. When I had a friend who could eat whatever she wanted and not gain weight I was jealous. Women with perfect hair, skin, teeth, and bodies became the enemy.

It wasn't until I decided to stop being jealous and embrace admiration that things began to change. When that changed, everything changed; I learned how to honor and be grateful for where I was. Today I am so grateful for my olive skin, brown eyes, wavy hair, muscular legs and slender arms. I have worked hard on my body and continue to do so. I am a work in progress and that is absolutely fine with me.

Use the Four-D Principle for Optimal Health

Decide to put your oxygen mask on first.

Define what optimal health means to you.

Dump any foods that make you feel bad, any lifestyle habits that are sabotaging your health, and anyone who is not supportive of your choice to become healthier.

Definitive Action: choose one or two health strategies to adopt every single month. Once you have mastered these, return to this chapter and choose one or two more. It is the little things repeated daily that truly create the greatest results.

Have It All Affirmation

My body is a miracle and I choose to be healthy and free.

- *HAVE IT ALL WOMAN* EMPOWERMENT EXERCISE -

Schedule It In!

As women we often put everyone before ourselves. When this goes on for long periods of time we can become exhausted, angry, and even ill. Before moving onto the next chapter, take some time to do the following:

- *Make an appointment for your next physical, including blood work and a pap smear.*
- *Perform a self-breast exam.*
- *Schedule in workouts.*
- *Schedule in a time once per week to create a meal plan.*
- *Schedule in your appointments for complementary care, such as acupuncture, massage, etc. for the next six months.*

CHAPTER FOUR

Step 4: Faith

"How do I love thee? Let me count the ways.
I love thee to the depth and breadth and height
My soul can reach, when feeling out of sight
For the ends of Being and ideal Grace.
I love thee to the level of everyday's
Most quiet need, by sun and candle-light.
I love thee freely, as men strive for Right;
I love thee purely, as they turn from Praise.
I love thee with a passion put to use
In my old griefs, and with my childhood's faith.
I love thee with a love I seemed to lose
With my lost saints, --- I love thee with the breath,
Smiles, tears, of all my life! --- and, if God choose,
I shall but love thee better after death."

— Elizabeth Barrett Browning, *Poet*

CHAPTER FOUR

Step 4: Faith

They Know Not What They Do

"If I am not, may God put me there; and if I am, may God so keep me."

—Joan of Arc, *Advocate*

When I was four years old, my mother and I lived in low-rent apartments in a somewhat unfavorable part of Halifax, Nova Scotia. There were many other children who lived in three adjacent buildings; we were a variable mixture of skin tones, languages and cultural mores. My mother was extremely religious and I was not allowed to wear pants as she thought that this was too provocative. Instead, I was forced to wear long, to the ankle, dresses that not only covered most of my body, but inhibited play.

I was often bullied at school and each day became one recurring nightmare after another. I dreaded going to school and I dreaded the long walk of vulnerability home where I would be harassed, chased and sometimes even beaten up.

My mother worked as a registered nurse and due to the shift work often left me alone. I was a "latchkey" kid. It was extremely lonely. I felt like an outcast and even more than that, I lived in terror most of the time. If my mother was home at night, I felt somewhat safe; however, it wasn't uncommon for her to go to work and leave me alone overnight, where I would cower in terror in the front hall closet fearing for my life.

During the week, and on weekends, we took the bus to church. It was a laying on of hands and fainting in the aisles kind of church, and ostensibly, I was a very good girl in that I didn't tell anyone that my mother was leaving me alone. People felt sorry for us. My mother told people what a cruel man my father was and how he had abandoned us, when the truth was that she had kidnapped me. Being so young, I honestly didn't know any different.

One thing that had been a constant in my life, from my earliest memories, was God. By the time we lived in Halifax, my mother had been a member of several churches and some operated more like cults. Despite the threats, the manipulation and the terror of living a sinful life and facing eternity in hell if I was bad, I continued to pray to God, understanding back then that religion and God are not necessarily the same thing.

By the time I was five my prayers to God had become more natural – not done out of fear or obligation but out of love. I honestly felt, and still feel, that God is with me always. I credit this belief for surviving one of the saddest experiences of my childhood.

It was a dusky afternoon and I was playing on the playground at our apartment complex. As usual, I was alone. When a parent asked where my mother was, I would lie and say she was inside even though she was at work. On this particular day, as I swung from the monkey bars, a group of children approached and asked me to play. I couldn't believe it. I felt so excited thinking that, at last, I was accepted.

They suggested that we go into the basement of one of the buildings and play hide and seek. I happily agreed, still blissful and the thought of being part of a group, and not just any group – this was the group of popular kids in our complex.

We snuck into the basement and just as I thought we were about to play, the children surrounded me. Suzanne, one of the girls, pulled out a rubber skipping rope and said, "Okay, let's whip her."

I felt bile rise up in my throat. My stomach turned over and my heart started racing. I had nowhere to run; there were too many kids. They all took turns with the lashes, which stung unbelievably. I could feel my skin burn and thought that there would soon be blood. As each child laughed and struck me, I remembered the story of Christ on the cross and said silently, "Forgive them for they know not what they do."

Immediately I felt a bright light surround me; it was blinding. I stopped feeling any pain and had the sensation of leaving my body. I could see the children whipping me but I felt nothing. I knew that God had come to protect me.

The children heard a noise and soon scattered, taking my shoes. I sat alone crying for a moment and then somehow found my way back to my apartment. I went inside and locked the door, weeping and fearing the children would come back. Although I told my mother what happened, she did nothing, telling me that God wants us to forgive.

Looking back on that day, I know that it was God's love that protected me. For years I resented my mother for not standing up for me, for not calling the parents of the children and continuing to leave me alone. Today, I have forgiven her too because, like the children, I am certain that she also knew not what she had done.

A Foundation in Faith

"Sometimes beautiful things come into our lives out of nowhere. We can't always understand them, but we have to trust in them. I know you want to question everything, but sometimes it pays to just have a little faith."

— Lauren Kate, *Author*

You may be wondering why faith is part of the solid base of a woman's *have it all* life – questioning why it is something to be considered at all when so many women measure success as having a healthy body, a great relationship and ample money. The reality is that life is going to throw us some curves. We are going to have defining moments where we face the death of a loved one, go through financial hardships, get diagnosed with an illness, deal with divorce or infidelity, a layoff, a downturn, abuse or any number of cataclysmic events. During these times, faith is truly one of the only things that will get you through and thus anchoring yourself in faith, and how you express that faith is of utmost importance to creating a well-balanced *have it all* life.

A survey of 18,000 people by Ipsos Social Research Institute found that approximately 51% of the world's population believes in God, while approximately

18% are undecided. When the definition of God is opened up to "a higher power," the number increases to significantly to over 80%. Furthermore, as evidenced by a 2008 report delivered to the Royal Economic Society, people who believe in God are much better able to deal with emotional stress such as divorce, death of a family member or being laid off. Research has also suggested that those who believe in God are happier overall.

There are approximately 21 major religions in the world. These religions are the expression of how one chooses to worship God. Wars, alienation and persecution have occurred over religion and yet the constant is a belief in God.

I cannot create evidence for you to believe that God exists if you do not share that notion; however, what I can tell you is that even those who formerly remained unconvinced, such as Dr. Eben Alexander, MD, author of the best-selling book Proof of Heaven, are now reconsidering their position after life-altering circumstances force them to experience God. There are countless stories of people experiencing God during near death-experiences: people who saw light, reconnected with deceased loved ones, or were guided through heaven only to be given answers to long-plaguing questions. To anyone who has gone through this, God, in all His forms, does exist.

As women, having a solid belief in God is going to lower our stress levels and create greater positive outcomes. When we can surrender our need to control things, let go of having to know why each and every thing happens, and take solace that yes, God indeed always has a bigger plan for us, then inherently we will experience greater peace and that peace, or surrender, is a beautiful launch pad to creating more in all areas of our lives.

Bringing More Faith Into Our Lives

"If you judge people, you have no time to love them." — Mother Teresa

I was once in Hong Kong, which is coincidentally one of my favorite places in the world, for business. When I am there I like to have Dim Sum at Ming Do, in

Admiralty. In addition to an incredible assortment of dishes, they have a mango dessert that is absolutely incredible. I love the kinetic energy of Hong Kong and the slight formality of the place. The people are fantastic.

While there I had arranged a business meeting with a colleague and she asked if she could invite two friends along. Matthew Ferry, the speaker and author, says, "Whatever is offered, say 'yes' and be a 'yes' to life." I am open to meeting new people so I agreed.

One of the women was named Elizabeth* and she was a striking lady of Chinese descent. Within minutes of our meeting her, she shared with us that she had a son. She then proceeded to ask me to guess how old her son was. I looked at Elizabeth, who appeared to be in her early thirties, and guessed that her son was four. She smiled a gorgeous beaming grin and said, "He is ten. How old do you think I am?"

I do not care if you're a man or woman; this is a loaded question. Guess too low and people know you are not sincere; guess too high and people are insulted. Looking at Elizabeth, I honestly guessed that she was about thirty-four. She laughed, leaning in and shared that she was actually "old," and that she was forty-four.

I was surprised. She looked great. I asked Elizabeth what she did as a way of finding out what she did to look so healthy. She shared that she worked half days and stayed at home with her son the other half. She shared that her husband worked long hours and that they had lost the magic in their marriage.

As lunch unfolded, Elizabeth confided that she was not happy. For the last fifteen years she had put everyone's needs before her own. She was stuck, frustrated and miserable. Looks can be deceiving, and in this case they were. Elizabeth also said that she felt too old to try something new. She was thinking of leaving her husband and was wrestling with that because of her strong Catholic faith.

I looked into those beautiful eyes and could see the pain beyond the beauty. From my heart, and my gut instinct, I told Elizabeth that she needed to live her life with more faith. She didn't have to know all of the answers and if she prayed to God to let her see herself as He saw her then she eventually would. Through tears she told me that I was the second person to tell her that very thing within the same number of days. I said, "Elizabeth, there is a message here for you."

Elizabeth promised me that she would have more faith. She also committed to having a conversation with her husband and working on bringing more faith into their marriage. She confessed that she was exhausted by trying to figure out her life and the sheer notion that she could surrender her troubles to God's hands brought her a degree of peace.

Like so many women, Elizabeth appeared to *have it all* on the outside – money, looks and a great marriage. The truth was that she was suffering and was so overwhelmed with trying to "figure things out" that it was taking an emotional toll on her. By simply remembering to live in faith, she changed her outlook and the last thing I heard, was much more optimistic and much better off.

We can bring more faith into our lives simply by reminding ourselves to surrender our problems to God. When we are stressed out, worried or overwhelmed, simply allowing ourselves to say a quick prayer like, "Thank you God for having this covered," is effective in releasing our challenges and garnering a different perspective. When we truly do not feel that we have to have all of the answers, the miracles begin to show up in our lives. The right people, the right circumstances and the solutions are made manifest by simply deciding that God is in control.

Create a Daily Ritual of Prayer and Meditation

"Beloved, let us love one another, for love is from God, and whoever loves has been born of God and knows God. Anyone who does not love does not know God, because God is love." —John 4:7-8

Something to consider is that many people speak and few listen. Furthermore, many people listen and few actually hear. When we pray, we do all of the talking. When we meditate, we do all of the listening. Prayer and meditation are forms of connecting with God at a deeper level. This allows us to experience a profound submersion in the infinite love of God.

If you have ever had this sensation then you can relate when I share that there is no feeling like it; to be with God, to feel God's infinite love and to be released of all judgments, fears and uncertainties. Some call this nirvana, which by one definition means to be free of all attachment. To some it is pure bliss, joy or absolute contentment. This is what I experienced as a child while the other children were whipping me; this is also what I experience daily in my prayer and meditation.

Prayer and meditation have been shown to have profound effects on healing. Studies actually show that people who pray are more likely to recover from life-threatening diseases and other health challenges. People who use mindfulness, a form of meditation, are more likely to lose weight. Furthermore, couples who believe in God and have a regular practice of prayer are less likely to divorce, and are much more satisfied as a couple, according to a 2011 study published in the journal Marriage and Family.

Creating a daily habit of prayer and meditation has proven effective for many women that I have worked with. They report greater peace, joy and harmony in their lives. One woman shared with me that daily meditation, done to a meditation audio available on my website, assisted her with quitting smoking after fourteen years. Another woman told me how the relationship with her mother improved dramatically after they both agreed to meditate daily using one of the meditations on my site. We have wonderful resources available on www.susansly.com.

We can always deepen our relationship with God. Begin today by choosing to simply pray. Surrender all of your challenges to God, and furthermore, thank God for all of the blessings in your life. Make time every day to meditate, even for five minutes. Sit in silence, take several deep breaths and simply meditate on the word "love."

It took me years to develop a meditation practice. I have prayed all of my life, but when it came to sitting in silence or doing a guided meditation, I did not really make it a priority most likely because I didn't see the benefit. Today, I begin each day with at least twenty minutes of meditation and prayer. My body is healthier, my thoughts are clearer, I am more even with my emotions and feel much greater fulfillment in my life.

We can meditate and pray anywhere – on the subway, on the airplane, even with our eyes open standing in line at the ATM. Connecting with God does not have to be contingent on location; it has everything to do with our ability to focus our intentions on Him regardless of where we are.

I encourage you to anchor your *have it all* life in daily prayer and meditation. It will change your life in beautiful and positive ways. Most importantly, our prayer and meditation defines our relationship with God; although we may also choose to attend church, synagogue, chapel or another house of worship once or more per week, it is our daily devotion that denotes our ability to lead a life where we are not paralyzed in fear of what we feel we cannot control.

Surrender the fears of your heart to God. Let go of what you perceive are circumstances beyond your control. As the saying goes, "Let go and let God." Through daily prayer and meditation you strengthen your faith and thus you let go and trust further in God; that in and of itself is a beautiful, cherished thing.

See Yourself as God Sees You

"Be very careful if you make a woman cry, because God counts her tears."

— From the Talmud

I once read an article about a woman who had released over one hundred pounds. Now, with sagging skin, she wrestled with the idea of having plastic surgery to cut away what would amount to several square feet of her body. This woman was young and had been raised in a devoutly Mormon home. Although several people were supportive, she felt as though she was betraying God.

Her struggle went on for months. At some point she wanted to get married and the thought of her future husband seeing her naked, with so much skin hanging from her body, caused her to feel shame and embarrassment; she didn't see how she could give herself freely being so self-conscious.

Finally, after counseling, consultations and prayer, the young woman decided to have the surgery. During the days leading up to the procedure her emotions vacillated between fear and excitement. The night before the surgery was the agonizing as the woman questioned if she had made the right decision. She got down on her knees to pray and asked God to please give her an answer – was she doing the right thing? A still small voice in her heart whispered, "See yourself as God sees you."

That night the young woman slept peacefully. The next day she had her surgery without complication. Since the surgery she has come to terms with the procedure and feels completely content in her decision.

Since reading this article, I too have prayed this same prayer understanding full well that God sees us as infinite, beautiful, Divine beings. By praying this prayer every day, you will soon find yourself making better choices in your life, having great teachers and mentors show up, and most of all you will come to a place of deeper self-love and appreciation. See yourself as God sees you.

Use the Four-D Principle for Faith

Decide to have a relationship with the Divine.

Define what that relationship looks like.

Delete any notion that you are less than perfect in God's eyes.

Definitive Action: develop a daily practice of prayer and meditation.

Have It All Affirmation

I am Divinely created and choose to see myself as God sees me.

- *HAVE IT ALL WOMAN* EMPOWERMENT EXERCISE -

Daily Prayer and Meditation

Find a special corner of your home to create a place that is sacred to you. You may choose to have photos of people you love, a book of prayer, cushions, and whatever else inspires you to surrender to love. Create time daily, preferably in the morning or in the evening, to go to your special place to pray and meditate. Take time to shut out the world and come to a place of Divine peace. This will transform your life.

Age 8—The 1970's were not the most fashion forward period of my life.

Me at 200 pounds.

Our first home.

With Margret, my accidental daughter.

Visiting a United Nations Refugee Camp in Malawi, Africa.

With my Have It All Sisters after the Disney Princess 1/2 Marathon.

Celebrating after another Boston Marathon—each race is a gift.

Renewing wedding vows in Bali with my best friend my husband, Chris.

Making a new friend while doing field work in Cambodia.

Chris and I riding an elephant in Angkor Wat.

Our family at the Elephant Preserve in Indonesia.

With one of my mentors, author of 7 NY Times Bestsellers, Harvey Mackay.

Lucky girl—with the infamous Larry King at his home in Los Angeles.

CHAPTER FIVE

Step 5: Self-Love

"When you're different, sometimes you don't see the millions of people who accept you for what you are. All you notice is the person who doesn't."

— Jodi Picoult, *Author*

CHAPTER FIVE

Step 5: Self-Love

The Epic Journey of Self-Love

"When a woman becomes her own best friend life is easier."

— Diane Von Furstenberg, *Designer*

Ronda Eva Harris was born on September 13th, 1953 in Brooklyn, New York. Before she completed her third year of life, Ronda's mother died; little Ronda went to live with her grandmother in a home of "nightmares." Sexually and physically abused, Ronda was the little girl that no one wanted.

Desperate to find and feel love, Ronda became pregnant by age sixteen. By the age of twenty-one she had three children and was married to a physically abusive husband. Like so many women who are sexually and physically abused, Ronda had mistaken sex for love and affection.

Several black eyes, broken ribs, a displaced uterus and severe depression led Ronda to attempt suicide. She ended up in a psychiatric ward, where she confessed how empty she felt in her life. Getting the courage to take her children, she wound up on welfare, where she remained for eight years until she applied to go to Medger Evers College. After three and a half years of part-time studies she finished summa cum laude.

Ronda went on to become a lawyer, a priestess and eventually a best-selling author, speaker and talk show host who counts Oprah Winfrey as one of her best friends. She changed her name to Iyanla Vanzant and has powerfully impacted millions of women around the world, including me.

What takes a woman from abused, battered and pregnant at sixteen to becoming a powerful inspirational speaker and transformational leader? Iyanla, in her many books, credits the decision to begin to love herself as the catalyst for the journey. As long as she stayed in self-loathing there would only be one outcome. The moment she decided to love herself enough to put one foot in front of the other and take steps to improve her life, the right people and the right circumstances appeared.

We Teach Others How to Treat Us

"I don't believe in guilt, I believe in living on impulse as long as you never intentionally hurt another person, and don't judge people in your life. I think you should live completely free." —Angelina Jolie, *Actress*

Many women allow people to steal their power. By putting ourselves last, we teach people that we are not important. We also attract people into our lives who support our misappropriated view that we are not worthy of love.

As women, we often have self-effacing thoughts: "I am not good enough, smart enough, pretty enough, capable enough, worthy enough," and so forth. These are all rooted in a lack of self-love. When we think these things we will attract into our lives people who reinforce our limiting self-belief as young Ronda did in the previous story.

The relationships I had, prior to my husband, were mere attractions of what I felt about myself. When I thought I was worthless, that I didn't matter and that I was not lovable, I attracted men who were abusive or apathetic. They were merely showing up in my life because that is what I thought I deserved. Before my husband, Chris, reappeared I had made a decision to begin to love myself. It wasn't easy and it was a definitive journey however it was a catalyst to the life I have now. In essence, how could anyone truly love me, if I didn't love myself?

It is assured that any challenging person who remains in your life will be there until you embrace self-love. Once you begin to love yourself, these people will either mystically change their behavior or simply disappear from your life altogether. People, you see, are simply mirroring back to us how we feel about ourselves; change the feeling and change the outcome.

Self-love and ego are not one in the same. To love ourselves is simply to make a decision to see the beauty within, to see ourselves as God sees us and to truly step into our own power. The ego and narcissism are to put ourselves above others – to feel elitist in some form.

The next time you look in the mirror, go beyond the surface and stare deeply into your own eyes. Look at this woman, full of experience, wisdom, and heart, and tell her that you love her. She is, after all, Divinely created and by loving her you further express your ability to love others. We can never give to someone else something that is not within ourselves.

Begin With Self-Respect

"An ounce of performance is worth pounds of promises."

— Mae West, *Performer*

As women we are very good at self-loathing. In fact, not only are we our worst critics, we are also extremely quick to criticize others. There are so many women who judge others, which is often symptomatic of their own insecurities. What we criticize in another woman can also be indicative of something we desire for ourselves and criticism is inherently a modality which deflects this longing.

In the chapter on health, we encountered Sarah, a woman who was focused on transforming her health. She was dedicated to her goals. Sarah chose to make healthier food choices, be disciplined with her eating and exercise regime, and most importantly, to respect herself enough to continue with those choices even in the face of ridicule.

The sad part was that many of Sarah's friends became critical when she began releasing weight. They said that they were worried she was losing the weight too fast and that she was unhealthy. The truth was that for every woman who criticized Sarah, there was a woman inside who envied Sarah's dedication and excellent habits. The most avid critic was a woman with high blood pressure who was, herself, sixty pounds overweight. Sarah's reply to all of these women was to point out that they didn't get overly concerned when she was obese.

When Sarah first started having success she thought that everyone would support her. Some of her most extreme critics were her "close" friends. What I counseled Sarah on was that it was imperative that she continue to respect her decisions and not to get caught up with what others were saying. From self-respect came self-love; Sarah loved herself enough to want to be healthy to be the mother and wife she had long dreamed of being. Once Sarah made this decision, new friends appeared and very soon Sarah had a new circle of people who shared her healthy habits.

Self-respect means building your own belief so that when people judge you, and they will, you are able to handle it with grace. Remember, some of the worst critics of your new habits will be people who are friends and family; regardless, choose to love them anyway.

Our "I AM" Statements

"Optimism is the faith that leads to achievement. Nothing can be done without hope and confidence." — Helen Keller, *Advocate*

The first step to change may appear to be very fundamental, yet it is extremely powerful. Oliver Wendell Holmes said, "Language is the blood of the soul out of which thoughts run and out of which they grow." What we think, creates how we feel, creates how we act, creates what we attract, and ultimately how we live our life. Our words are powerful and in essence what we say influences how we feel about ourselves.

Self-love must begin with our words. Putting ourselves down will ultimately cause us to feel bad and we will attract, as mentioned, those that support our limiting beliefs. Dr. Wayne Dyer, author of numerous best-selling books, says that when we use the words "I am" we actually invoke the name of God, and that by following "I am" with anything that is not positive is to blaspheme.

Only once in the scriptures does God give His name. In Exodus 3:14, God speaks to Moses from the burning bush and Moses asks to know the name of the One who is sending him. The Lord speaks and says, "I am that I am."

So often, as women, we will follow our "I am" statements with words such as "fat, stupid, worthless, lazy, incompetent, dumb, ugly," and so forth. We invoke the name of The Lord and of course will live into exactly what we say we are. To love ourselves is to release the urge to follow our "I am" statements with anything other than "beautiful, loving, kind, competent, intelligent, remarkable, magnificent," and so forth. As we invoke this simple act, we speak the word of God, and as it is written in Matthew 7:7, "Ask and it shall be given." In other words, as we follow our "I am" statements with positives we are asking to live into those qualities.

Deflection and Justification

"The more you praise and celebrate your life, the more there is in life to celebrate." — Oprah Winfrey, *Media Personality*

As we grow into awareness of self-love it becomes apparent that we must also choose to accept love in all forms. One of these forms is a genuine compliment: a lover, a friend, a child or family member who authentically praises us for something we have done, who we are or how we look. Sadly, many women deflect these comments. This creates two outcomes, the first being that the compliments become fewer and eventually stop, and the second being that we are, in essence, calling the originator of the compliment a liar.

Many women complain that their partners have stopped genuinely complimenting them. They feel unloved and unappreciated. In the majority of these cases the partner has stopped because the woman has deflected the praise. For example, a husband may say, "Honey, you look beautiful." The woman may say, "No I don't, I am still twenty pounds overweight." To him, she is beautiful. To her, he is lying and many women perceive such compliments as a tactic for the man to get her in bed.

Sadly, even if the intent was simply a compliment to his wife, the man is now rejected. Our human nature is to protect ourselves from pain and condemnation, so although he may compliment his wife in the future, he will be more cautious, and if she continues to deflect his compliments, will eventually stop.

Another way we deflect is to justify. Have you ever had a girlfriend compliment your outfit and you had to justify it in some way? An example would be your friend saying, "Wow, that outfit is amazing," and you say, "Yes, I go it on sale for half price." You could simply say, "thank you;" however, you felt that in some way you had to justify the price. Many women do this as well.

As women we are not always adept at receiving anything, let alone compliments. Many women are great givers and extremely poor receivers and this only serves to create disharmony as we embark on a journey of self-love. Loving ourselves is the catalyst for being lovable, and receiving love and praise from others will ultimately allow us to stand in greater appreciation of the woman in the mirror.

The next time your partner, your child, your friend, family member, or even stranger compliments you, simply say, "thank you." Release the need to justify or deflect. Choose to become a great receiver of praise, understanding full well that in order for us to fully love and give love we must also be able to receive love.

Our Words are Powerful

"Nothing is impossible; the word itself says 'I'm possible'!"

— Audrey Hepburn, *Actress*

Mother Teresa was once asked to be in an anti-war rally. She said, "If you change it to a peace rally let me know and I will be there." Mother Teresa felt that to be against anything was to create more negative energy. To be for something is to create positive energy. By being for peace, she was moving forward. To be against war would be staying still or moving backward.

Your words will attract whatever you want, so use the language of success. Speaking in favor of something, as opposed to being against something, sends a clear message that you want a positive outcome. This is also a more loving stance to take. Instead of saying something such as "don't get sick," you can say "stay well." Instead of "watch that you don't get hurt," you can say "stay safe." By focusing on a positive outcome, we turn the thoughts away from any potentially negative effect.

As you go through your day, observe your words. Speak powerfully positive words over others and over yourself. Ultimately as we shift our language, we shift our life.

If It Makes You Feel Bad – Dump It

"I would always rather be happy than dignified."

— Charlotte Brontë, *Author*

Stand in line at any grocery store, observing the covers of magazines, and you will receive a host of competing messages all meant to attract your attention. One magazine may feature a title such as, "Secrets of how the stars get thin," while another may have feature an impossibly time-demanding, perfect chocolate cake. The messages we are sent, as women, are really centered on an intangible ideal that suggests we must be reed-thin, gourmet chefs, be great in the bedroom, walk in six-and-a-half-inch heels while we play with our children at the playground and keep an immaculate home. In many ways women have been taught that having it all is impossible because the media directs us to focus on things that are superficial, staged and rarely accomplished by one woman.

Undoubtedly the cake on the cover of the magazine was created by a well-trained pastry chef. Impossibly thin celebrities have teams of personal trainers, food delivery, make-up artists, stylists and can be air-brushed into an implausible form with flawless skin, perfect breasts, lean thighs and a flat stomach. It is not the fault of the celebrities – in fact, many have spoken openly about the demands of Hollywood—it is the insatiable hunger of the public, the women buying the magazines, for perfection. It leaves me to question whether or not we actually do want to feel bad.

A 2004 study done by Hawkins , Richards , Granley , and Stein at the Center for Change in Orem, Utah exposed college-aged girls to media images of models.

The girls were found to feel dissatisfaction, negative mood states, lowered self-esteem and exhibit greater tendency to consider an eating disorder.

In essence, many women are purchasing these magazines—and I admit to buying them myself—only to end up feeling inadequate. Perhaps a cautionary label might read, "Only purchase if you have a healthy self-esteem." If you are wrestling with being able to love yourself, I urge you to take a break from any media that causes you to feel bad. Do not watch television that features women who are impossibly thin or read magazines with so much airbrushing that even the featured actresses do not recognize themselves. If something causes you to feel bad or inadequate, dump it either permanently or until you feel so strongly about your self-worth that you can simply be entertained by such media.

Lastly, as we foray into the next level of our life pyramid we will explore relationships. In this chapter we will also contemplate letting go of toxic friendships: people who cause us to feel bad. We are meant to feel good. We are meant to be deeply in love with ourselves and have an infinite well of love to draw from and pour out into the world. When we feel "less than" or "not enough" we are not able to fully give of ourselves. Make a decision to let go of anything that is not in alignment with self-love and you will quickly find that it is easier and easier to look into the mirror and fall madly, deeply in love with the woman you see.

Use the Four-D Principle for Self-Love

Decide to commit to the journey of loving yourself.

Define ways in which to express that love.

Dump anything that causes you to feel bad.

Definitive Action: create a book or journal of self-appreciation.

Have It All Affirmation

I love myself at all times and under all circumstances.

- *HAVE IT ALL WOMAN* EMPOWERMENT EXERCISE -

Self-Love

Take a few minutes and recall anything positive that anyone has ever said about you. Write these things down. If you are struggling with this, then conversely, consider all of the negative things you say about yourself and write down the opposite. For example, if you say, "*I am fat*," then write, "*I am fit*." Once you have ten items, make your "I AM" list and write it on a recipe card. Tape this to your bathroom mirror. First thing in the morning, and last thing at night, read your "I AM" list. At first it may be challenging to believe those "I AM" statements; however, after several repetitions these will become more natural and you will be living into the notion of how God sees you.

CHAPTER SIX

Step 6: Fulfilling Relationships

"When a woman becomes her own best friend life is easier."

— Diane Von Furstenberg, *Designer*

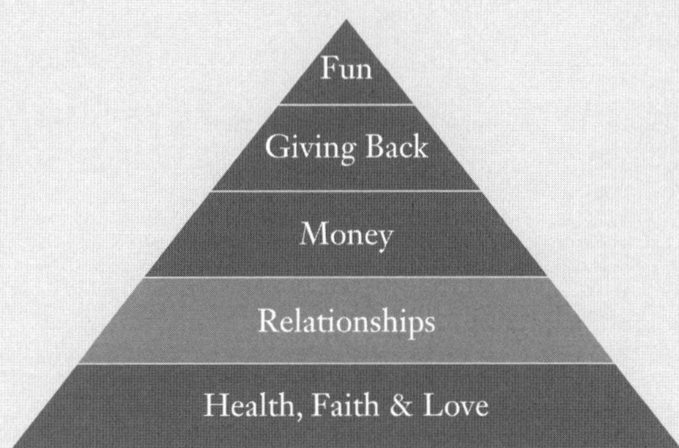

CHAPTER SIX

Step 6: Fulfilling Relationships

The Accidental Relationship

"If you look at what you have in life, you'll always have more. If you look at what you don't have in life, you'll never have enough."

— Oprah Winfrey, *Television Personality*

In late March of 2009 I travelled to Malawi. I was six and a half months pregnant with our fourth child and I had no idea why I had come back to this country fuelled by poverty and made famous by the patronage of Madonna. It was hot, I was hot and everyone around me shuffling, shoving and positioning themselves in the queue were also hot. The customs line was an hour long, and with large men and imperious women jostling for position in the so-called line I thought to myself, "T.I.A. – this is Africa;" a line from Leonardo Dicaprio's movie Blood Diamond.

My husband would tell you that I get wanderlust. Although my home and my family are my anchor – my personal docking station, if you will – it doesn't take more than a few weeks at home before I begin to look longingly at the Travel Section in my Sunday New York Times or stray aimlessly through the travel books at our local bookstore. I come from a family of wanderers on my Dad's side: Chinese who ventured to Jamaica, the United States and places all over the world. My Aunt Ruth and Uncle Mike have had many adventures circumventing the globe and living for a year or two in places like Manila, Bombay, Kazakhstan, Hong Kong and others; now in their seventies they resign themselves to writing travel guides about China and going on archaeological digs in places like Jordan.

Growing up I did not have the privilege of much travel, though I could lay claim to visiting both California's Disneyland and Florida's Disney World. I made a pact with myself that I would one day roam the world and gift myself with a global education. Although I have many, many more places to visit, I consider myself blessed to have experienced a near-death plane ride flying into the jungle in Guatemala and tasted the most divine Pizza Margherita in Rome. I love the smell of rich history at the British Museum in London and the pain-wrenching reflexology in the basement of a store in Hong Kong. The more I travel, the more I want to travel and I openly admit that some of my ideas are not so lovingly welcomed.

On this particular visit to Africa with my baby bump being bustled and my nerves being jostled I once again asked why I was here. Wanderlust aside, my friend Jim had begged me not to go. Chris was less than impressed that I had chosen now, in my condition, pregnant with our child, to globetrot from Cambodia to Malawi to Rome and then home. I argued that it was book research, a story of the perils of impoverished girls in Cambodia and Africa and their risk for sex trafficking. Meanwhile, both Chris and I knew that the book was not the primary reason for my misadventures; the reality is that aside from being with my children, my husband, communing with God and running, the Third World is a place where I feel truly alive.

Really, I had come to Africa to refuel and regain perspective. I have a beautiful life and I am extremely grateful. Every day I have the opportunity to inspire people as an act of service. I have the honor and privilege to assist people in discovering the beautiful person that lies within. I have worked hard to get to where we are and I continue to do so. In my relationship with myself I have strived to release proving, self-loathing and competition to produce from a place of absolute peace, trust and surrender. This isn't always easy in business and it is easy to lose perspective at times.

In Africa, none of the rest of the world matters. In Africa, you are in Africa and that is a statement in and of itself. The smell of burning wood is what welcomes me on this visit. People are preparing to cook their evening meal and although Malawi has very little shrubbery remaining in its capital, Lilongwe, people find it anyway. The ride from the airport is met with a variety of sensory stimuli: a child playing naked by the road with a distended belly, or a gaunt man, looking twenty years his own senior, riding a bike in a tattered blazer, pants and ratty shoes.

Upon entering the capital, one is met with paved roads, homes behind walls where gardens full of flowers and vegetables are planted. There are a few embassies and even a modern grocery store. One could be wrongly lulled into a false delusion that this is normal – that everyone drives in cars and has a full belly at night. No. A short drive away, children die of malaria and only know hunger, a tormented ache in their belly, that is experienced for the majority of their life. No, T.I.A. and everyone knows that the only hope is found in the foreigners; thus, the majority of people staying at our hotel are indeed just that – well-meaning people like myself, who are only perhaps slightly more enlightened than someone who has never been here.

A day after my arrival, Jones, a social worker at an orphanage run by friends from Canada, called me to say that he had found a girl for me to interview for my book. He said that this girl had survived a brutal rape and was now living in a women's shelter in town. She had given permission to be interviewed by me.

Sandy, my Executive Assistant and also my angel, and I went to the shelter to meet Margret, a beautiful 15-year-old girl with soulful eyes that betrayed a depth of life experience that no mother would ever wish for a daughter. Margret reported that she liked school. She woke up early every morning to clean the latrines at the shelter. Most mornings her bed was covered with cockroaches which were as large as small mice. Margret walked about four miles to and from school; in the evening there were more chores and homework.

I asked her about her feelings of her life and a grin overtook her face when she replied through her translator that she would rather be here than living with her uncle, the uncle who had brutally raped her, stolen her virginity and impregnated her. She would rather be away from the aunt who threw her out naked and tossed all of her clothes in the latrine pit. Margret, in her cockroach-invested shelter, was much happier and dreamed of being an accountant and going to university. Her greatest desire was an education.

Margret is now my fifth child and we are her guardians. Malawian laws prohibit the adoption of Malawian children by foreigners who have not resided in the country for a minimum number of years. Yes, exceptions have been made, though often for political or financial reasons. We send Margret, an orphan (both her parents died of HIV), to a girls' boarding school and hope one day to bring her to North America to be educated.

I went to Africa to research a book and I came home with a partial daughter. What I have learned over time is that our richest relationships are those that are unexpected. The most amazing friendships and partnerships are perhaps the very ones that have not even occurred yet. We definitely attract people into our lives for a reason. Sometimes this reason is not apparent in the instance; however, every person does indeed have a gift to offer us—a lesson which is going to enrich our lives by teaching us something about ourselves.

Our 100th Birthday

"Once you figure out who you are and what you love about yourself, I think it all kinda falls into place." —Jennifer Aniston, *Actress*

When we come to the end of this lifetime we will not wish we had more material wealth; instead, we will be focused only on the relationships we had and the experiences that came as a result of those relationships. Take a moment to imagine your one hundredth birthday. See yourself sitting in front of your birthday cake aglow with candles. Look around the room at the smiling faces. Who is standing there and how do they feel about you?

Dealing with our own mortality is bittersweet. On one hand, we understand that the passing of our physical body is inevitable; on the other hand we have the opportunity to make every juicy second count. The truth is that our time is limited and we cannot waste one day in hate, anger, judgment or guilt.

People will come and go in and out of our lives. Some of these people will be perceived as positive, while others may be perceived as negative. The perception is your choice; when you realize that every person has something to teach us there can be no negativity – only contribution, which is beautiful in and of itself.

Our relationships reflect back to us the inner workings of our soul. People who have many rich relationships tend to be well-balanced, loving and self-assured. People who lack rewarding relationships tend to be selfish, controlling, arrogant and are secretly deeply hurting inside. Those capable of hurting another are dealing with their own deep self hurts.

When we decide to become more self-loving and honor our true self, our relationships shift. New people come into our lives to support our new way of being and others disappear from our lives, their work done – often a catalyst for us to change.

Ultimately, we have the power to create our relationships. We are capable of surrounding ourselves with people who love and support our dreams. In order to attract more and more incredible people into our lives we must first decide to be the person we would want a relationship with; a person worth having at our one hundredth birthday.

It's Complicated

"Why does a woman work ten years to change a man, then complain he's not the man she married?" — Barbra Streisand, *Actress and Singer*

As women, we tend to think in terms of cause and effect; inherently we weigh the degree of our actions against how they will impact our relationship. Dr. John Gray, PhD, suggests that women have more synapses between the left and right hemispheres of our brains. Because of this, our thought patterns are not as linear as a man's. A woman will consider how her activities affect all of her primary relationships, whereas men tend to see the action, take the action and then think about how that action affects others.

Perhaps this goes back to our hunter-gatherer days when a man's primary role was to find food and not to think about how his emotions are affecting his family, how long he is away from his family finding this food or how his use of violence (the act of killing an animal) is impacting his daughter's life. Today, many men seek to be more sensitive and are encouraged to express their emotions; however, this also serves to lower their dopamine levels, which also lower testosterone. Even though we are evolved as a society, we are still wired as though it is ten thousand years ago.

Women are wired to be nurturers. We are programmed to express our feelings, to consider others and to protect our children. In today's society, where over seventy percent of mothers work outside the home, the demands are changing. Women are expected to produce like men, shelve emotions, and yet somehow manage to be considerate, kind and compassionate. These mixed messages are causing many women to be confused about their relationships and how to operate within those relationships.

I know many smart, self-confident, financially comfortable women who struggle to find a partner. Their lament is that many men want a trophy wife or a woman who needs him in some way. The challenge these independent women face is the ability to surrender at the end of the day and allow the man to do what he does best – solve problems and provide. It is definitely a dance.

Additionally, with social media women are in more relationships than ever before. It is mentally exhausting to be worried about your family and read a post by a long-lost college friend that she has lost her spouse. Women are wired to be concerned with the well-being of others, regardless of how we express it. Society has placed us in an unparalleled predicament in that we are inundated by what we feel is expected of us and what we are naturally programmed to do.

Today, more than ever before, our relationships are complicated. We have online and offline relationships. We have relationships that are unique to a group, club or social circle. We have relationships with our relatives. We have business relationships. Thanks to social media, we can even have relationships with people we have never met.

Many women take their smart phone, tablet or laptop to bed just so they can stay connected right up until the last minute. Other women eschew conventional dating altogether in hopes of finding the perfect partner online. It used to be that we met someone in person and sized up their merit. Today we judge a person by their profile, and truthfully, that isn't always accurate.

As women, the biggest challenges we face are making a decision of who is important in our lives, how we want to interact with people, who to stay in relationships with, how to maintain current relationships and make ourselves somewhat available to all of our social media contacts. In other words…it's complicated.

Just Because We Share DNA Doesn't Make it T.U.A.

"You show people what you're willing to fight for when you fight your friends."

— Hillary Clinton, *Former Secretary of State*

It has been said that our capacity to have deep, meaningful, trusting relationships is ultimately limited to only a handful of people. This ability is dependent upon two key factors: one being time and the other being investment. To have close, personal relationships requires nurturing of these connections and a fundamental ability to invest of ourselves including our trust, unconditional love and acceptance of the other.

These deep, powerful relationships are generally had with people with whom we have shared experience or history. We have witnessed these people at their worst – crying, angry, upset, and hurt – and have continued to love them. In turn, these people have observed us in our lowest states and stayed by our side through it all.

As previously referenced, in 1943, noted psychologist Abraham Maslow created a paper entitled A Theory of Human Motivation. In it he described our hierarchy of needs, asserting that once our fundamental physiological needs were met, including food, water, shelter and so forth, we would ascend to self-actualization. In that self-actualization we seek to love and be loved; we search for fulfilling intimate relationships.

Evidence has substantiated that to have a handful of people in our lives whom we can trust and have an authentic relationship with, these types of relationships will increase our chances of survival. People who are happily married, for example, have higher survival rates for diseases such as cancer. Women who have other close female friends are, in fact, happier; women connecting with women induces serotonin, a neurochemical which elicits overall feelings of joy. In other words, we do require a few close people in our lives to enhance our overall experience.

An impromptu poll on my Facebook Fan Page asking people to share their total number of "inner circle" relationships yielded an average number of five, which aligns with our capacity to invest time and effort into such relationships. I have heard these relationships best described as T.U.A., Total Unconditional Acceptance. As one friend described it – you walk into a room and your friend is standing over a body with a smoking gun in her hand and you say, "Who killed this person?" Graphic imagery aside, a great question to consider is how many people you truly have this kind of relationship with.

Draw a circle and write down the names of your T.U.A. friends and family members (just because you share DNA, doesn't make it T.U.A.) within the circle. These are your inner circle relationships; these are the relationships we not only want to nurture – they are, according to Maslow, critical to our survival.

I once knew a woman who was fully blind. She lived on her own in Chicago. She frequented a daily training call I did that was also attended by hundreds of others. We all knew her by her first name and little else. Sadly, one day this woman fell in her apartment and could not get up. She died alone. There was no one to help her. Can you imagine being blind, unable to get help, and eventually dying all by yourself? This woman did not have any T.U.A. relationships and she died a slow death with no one there.

As we contemplate who is in our T.U.A. circle we can also choose to have an outer circle; P.U.A. – Partially Unconditional Acceptance. These relationships are generally conditional on being part of a particular group or organization. For example, you may have someone at work who would bend over backward for you, and you in turn, but you may not have a strong relationship with this person outside of the office.

For some, these P.U.A. relationships occur within their church, a social club, a sports league, alumni association or even within a family. Our T.U.A. relationships, on the other hand, transcend all areas of our lives. Draw a second circle, an outer circle, and list your P.U.A. relationships. You will most likely have at least two or three times the number of people within this circle. These relationships are also important to foster as professional, physical and emotional success is most likely enhanced by these associations.

Look at your contacts and ask yourself who is a "yes" in your life. For example, if you have a critical task, require a reference or even someone to give guidance on a personal matter, who will answer the phone when they see your number? These are your P.U.A. people and ultimately having these types of relationships within the various aspects of our lives is also critical to our *have it all* journey; we will never *have it all* if we are trying to do it alone.

A Beautiful Relationship is Often Based on Hard Work

"A kiss is a lovely trick designed by nature to stop speech when words become superfluous." — Ingrid Bergman, *Actress*

My friend Kathy Smith has been married for over 28 years, and has seven beautiful children and several grandchildren. She and her husband, Tom, work together and are partners in life as well as business. At the Smith house there is always something going on. There are family dinners, football games to attend and people dropping by. Theirs is a very busy and fulfilling life.

When I attend functions with Kathy, she and Tom are always holding hands. When Kathy speaks, Tom looks at her in the same way that I am sure he did when they were in high school. Likewise, when Tom speaks, Kathy absolutely glows. To witness them speak of their children or their grandson is a sight to behold. Both Kathy and Tom light up.

Kathy has also had her trials and tribulations. Before becoming successful entrepreneurs Kathy ran a daycare out of her home and Tom was a butcher. In addition to their regular jobs, Kathy worked midnights at a grocery store, while Tom ran a paper route in the morning. Not only did they have little time for one another, they were constantly under financial stress.

With seven children, college tuition fees, insurance, groceries, school fees and activities there was very little money. The Smiths were living paycheck to paycheck, and that forced them to work hard on their relationship during the tough times. Kathy says that what brought them through was their faith in God.

Although they now have ample income, they are no happier than they were then, according to Tom. The biggest secret is that they choose to support and love one another no matter what was going on. When they eventually did transcend their financial challenges, they had already built a solid foundation in their relationship that only served to be enhanced by what they now have.

The bottom line is that when it comes to relationships, it is easy to be happy when everything is going well. When times are tough it is also easy to blame the other person, threaten to leave, end it all and just give up. Good relationships, whether these are with a partner, child, relative, friend or colleague, take work.

You may argue, you may disagree and ultimately you may get hurt; this doesn't mean you give up. You can choose to work harder; you can choose to become the person you would want to be in a relationship with. We all have areas in which we can grow and the healthiest of relationships are those where people can grow together.

Relationships are Dynamic

"You want me to act like we've never kissed, you want to forget; pretend we've never met, and I've tried and I've tried, but I haven't yet … You walk by, and I fall to pieces." — Patsy Cline, *Singer*

Relationships are dynamic and multifaceted. There is the relationship we have with our lover or partner, the relationship we have with our children, our family, our friends, our colleagues, employees and people we meet on a daily basis. These are people whose lives we impact without even realizing it. The most important dynamic is the relationship we have with ourselves.

I have learned that we never know how a relationship will evolve or who we will become within that relationship. Sometimes it starts and then diminishes only to be rekindled years later. Other times we meet someone and have amazing chemistry only to have the relationship fizzle out. Some of my closest friends are people with whom I have overcome challenges with and we have grown stronger together.

Some women are big risk takers when it comes to relationships, and completely give of themselves every time. Other women tend to be more cautious and these women I refer to as "islands." "Island" women do not let anyone in fully, nor do they allow others to contribute to them. Other women compartmentalize their relationships, whereby they have certain people they do certain things with, and only a handful of people in their inner circle.

Regardless of how we are being it is important to understand that all relationships are dynamic. We may enter into a relationship with caution only to find ourselves surrendering to passion. Conversely, we may begin a relationship giving fully of ourselves, only to pull back for some reason. Humans are complex; a multitude of factors enter into how we think, feel, act and express ourselves. Thus, relationships are even more complex as now we add all of the extraneous factors influencing our operating systems and multiply that, exponentially, by the number of people involved in the relationship.

When something is ever-changing, and ever-evolving, it is interesting. As human beings it is in our nature to evolve – to shift and to grow. Thus relationships must also evolve to reflect the changes of the individuals. If you have children then you can appreciate the notion that as much as they go from infant to toddler to preschooler to grade school and beyond, there is a small part of us that will forever see the child as our baby.

The same is true within a primary romantic relationship. In the beginning, we are in a "courting phase," perhaps choosing to be interested in things we wouldn't otherwise take notice of, laughing at jokes we do not really find funny, making an extra effort in our appearance and giving of ourselves more freely in the bedroom. As the "newness" of the relationship leaves, the tendency is to lose interest as opposed to looking for innovative ways to keep things fresh. This is a key cause of affairs; the majority of people who cheat on their partner report that it is because they no longer find them interesting.

No relationship is ever going to stay exactly the same and this is a good thing. All relationships are dynamic and we can either embrace this fact, choose to be creative in keeping our relationships fresh, or we can sta[illegible]e and potentially lose that thing which we once cherished.

Relationships are Dynamic

"Well, it seems to me that the best relationships—the ones that last—are frequently the ones that are rooted in friendship. You know, one day you look at the person and you see something more than you did the night before; like a switch has been flicked somewhere. And the person who was just a friend is ... suddenly the only person you can ever imagine yourself with."

— Gillian Anderson, *Actress*

Relationships provide a mirror of who we really are. Through others we can see ourselves as totally beautiful or possibly negative. We consistently attract people to us who reflect back to us precisely how we feel, including our deepest fears and insecurities. In Dr. Iyanla Vanzant's story we witnessed a woman who went from abusive relationship to abusive relationship because she did not love herself; her lack of self-worth attracted these men to her.

In my own life, I attracted relationships that reaffirmed how I felt about myself; not just with my romantic relationships, also with friends. Because I was so insecure about my looks, I attracted friends who pointed out the areas that I was most self-conscious of. In high school I had size nine feet by grade ten and my best friend liked to call me "canoe shoes." I was always hyper aware of my foot size and then after four babies, I became a size eleven. Not only did I attract criticism, I attracted larger feet.

As a child, I was extremely self-conscious of my skin color and my weight so I attracted people who made fun of both of those things. On a deeper level, I ached on the inside because I thought I wasn't lovable; the product of both parents each having two failed marriages, I attracted men who reinforced just how unlovable I was.

As women, we may think we are hiding our insecurities, but we are doing the opposite. We are magnetizing people to us who will point out every flaw we feel we have. Furthermore, like attracts like and we will attract people who behave exactly as we do. If we are complainers we will attract complainers. If we are gossiping, we will attract others who gossip with us and about us.

Every relationship we have is an opportunity to grow. People will either teach us how or how not to be. When we attract people into our lives who are critical we must ask ourselves if what they are saying is hurtful because at some level we feel the same way. If we find ourselves surrounded by people who are cruel or spiteful then we may wish to take a good solid look in the mirror and ask ourselves if we also engage in these behaviors.

All people have a gift to offer us, if we choose to see it. The gift may be in the form of highlighting an area that we want to reconcile or it may be in the form of teaching us a valuable lesson of what not to do.

I met a man on an airplane and we struck up a conversation. He was gushing about how wonderful his wife was. They had been married for almost twenty years. The miraculous part of this was that his wife was the daughter of a woman who had been married to or lived with eighteen men in the span of her daughter's upbringing. The odds were not in favor of this man and his wife having a long-term marriage; however, his wife used her mother's behavior as a lesson of how not to be.

If we stop and choose to see the gift in everyone, we can use these gifts to create fulfilling, substantial and loving relationships in our own lives. All people come from the Divine, and although they may be acting in ways that are not in alignment with this divinity it is merely a reflection of their humanness. Starting now, silently acknowledge everyone you come in contact with, from the homeless person on the street to the annoying co-worker, and see the divinity in that person. As you begin to do this, the hurtful, spiteful people will either leave your life or transform, because in seeing the divinity in others we are now able to see it in ourselves.

The Three J's

"Above all, be the heroine of your life, not the victim."

— Nora Ephron, *Author*

I once worked with a woman who complained to me that everyone in her sales team wasn't doing anything. She said that they were all talk and no action. I suggested to her that she pick up a mirror and speak the words into it that she was saying about her team. After doing this she called me back in tears realizing that it wasn't about the sales force, it was about her. She was judging her group; however, the reality was that she was simply projecting her own self-judgment.

Judgment is one of the three J's, which also include justification and jealousy. These are relationship killers and once we enter into this kind of behavior we lower ourselves and we absolutely magnetize more of the same to us. What the woman didn't know was that her sales team had come to me complaining about her leadership and that they were saying the exact same things about her, that she was saying about them. Judgment doesn't travel alone; the team was justifying their lack of results by blaming her leadership.

As women, we can be our own worst enemies; watch reality television and you will see the point exactly. Women are the harshest critics of other women and it is because women are the harshest critics of themselves. Much criticism comes down to jealousy, which is a wasted, low-calibrating emotion because it essentially points to a notion that we feel we are incapable of achieving something similar. For example, if your friend gets a new handbag, and you are jealous it is because at some level you feel that you will not be able to afford a bag like that.

Justification is when we try to make excuses for our situation, almost apologetically, deflecting responsibility away from ourselves. In relationships, women use this to justify an unhappy marriage, a child's lack of good behavior, being involved with people that we really do not want to be, and so forth. We justify almost every aspect of our lives.

As women we may complain about our circumstances; however, if we are not ready to take action we follow up our complaints by justifying our lives. I was once on a phone call with a person who was complaining about every part of her life and after I hung up, I was now frustrated and irritated; I had allowed myself to spend almost an hour listening to the complaining.

My daughter, Avery, was five at the time and she asked what was wrong. I explained that the person, on the other end of the phone, had been complaining to me. Avery said, "Mommy, do you know what happens to complainers?" "No," I replied. She said, "God makes them go back and learn the lesson all over again." It was wonderful wisdom then and it is wonderful wisdom now. When we complain, we will continue to learn our lessons until we stop justifying our circumstances and take action on changing our reality.

Begin right now. Let go of the three J's. There is no need to be jealous, to judge another or to justify your life. These emotions will poison your relationships and ultimately attract negative people into your life. It may be tough to stop gossiping, to stop judging and to stop having so many opinions about others, but how is this really serving you?

Author and noted speaker Sam Richter suggests that when it comes to voicing our opinions we imagine that what we want to say is printed on the front page of the New York Times for everyone to see. Would we still say it? Of course not. The truth is that once we voice or post any opinion of another, it becomes public regardless of how confidential we believe it to be. Almost everything we say about someone else is shared; the question is, if you knew the person you were speaking about truly understood how you felt would you still say it? Furthermore, if someone said the same thing about you, and they will, would you still be operating with judgment, jealousy or justification?

Life is much too short to let the three J's rule your life and be a cancer of your soul. Let them go right now and observe how quickly your world transforms.

A Loving Heart

"Kind words can be short and easy to speak, but their echoes are truly endless."

— Mother Teresa

Imagine, if you will, a love so pure and without conditions that by simply being in that presence we are absolved of any of our old hurts or perceptions of things we have done wrong. Visualize basking in this love until you felt so complete that you were then, in turn, able to go forward with love for all living things? How powerful would that be? How would that transform your world: to no longer express judgment, jealousy, and justification or any emotion that weakened your soul?

Mother Teresa said, "I have found the paradox, that if you love until it hurts, there can be no more hurt, only more love." This begs the question, if we all allowed ourselves to be more loving, how would the world transform? Could there be any pain or suffering if all things were done from love as opposed to anything else? That may perhaps seem like a utopian society; however, this notion that love can heal all has been written about through the ages.

The thirteenth century poet Rumi wrote, "Your task is not to seek for love, but merely to seek and find all the barriers within yourself that you have built against it." Within most people, myself included, are a series of barriers that prohibit us from loving fully, without conditions. These barriers, erected through a myriad of hurts and disappointments, have been cause to never fully give ourselves over to love. We may love; however, our love comes with conditions that create a variance in the degree of our love.

If you are a parent, you love your child unconditionally. As parents, we also know that as that child grows and perhaps makes decisions we do not agree with, we do not stop loving them; however, the love becomes more complicated as our worries and fears for our child overshadow the pure love that once was. When they were young we cradled them in our arms and told them how much we loved them; then, as they grew the "I love you's" became less frequent but were perhaps even more necessary.

If your child feels challenging to you, when was the last time you simply said, "I love you," without condition? What would happen if you texted them, told them or messaged them a simple, "I love you," without any need for anything in return? What would happen if more and more parents did this? What kind of generation would we raise?

I once attended an event with Dr. Wayne Dyer. He shared a story about visiting with his friend who has a young autistic son. While the mother rested, Wayne took the boy out for the afternoon. He swam with him, he held him and all the while repeated, "I love you." This child has been "difficult" and requires a great deal of energy. After two hours of hearing "I love you," the boy was calmer, happier and more self-assured.

My own son has been in the autistic spectrum and many worried about him. He was late to talk, to read, to walk and still cannot ride a bicycle at the age of ten.

One constant in his life is love. From the moment he wakes up to the moment he goes to bed, I tell him how much I love him. I send him love notes in his lunch. He knows he is loved and the interesting thing is that all of the teachers, therapists and support people in his life consistently remark that they have never seen a child with these challenges be so confident. Even as I write these words, I am reminded to commit to being even more loving to my children.

In our primary relationship it is easy to see how we begin to slide the scale of demise not long after we take our vows. In the early stages, there are perhaps love notes, love texts, words spoken of love and showers of love that seem so infinite that one is giddy basking in the endless sea of love. Then children come or perhaps one struggles to conceive and there are fewer "I love you's." As attention leans toward life and kids perhaps the daily "I love you's" cease and resentment builds as there appears to be a finite amount of love to give; we forget that our ability to love is endless, and like any muscle that requires flexing, it is something we must do every day as opposed to just on special occasions or conditionally such as after "making love."

We were created by a loving God. We were given the ability to love openly. In many cases we have forgotten this and spend a great degree of time and energy trying to find that blissful feeling of love when, in fact, we have had it within all along. As we begin to be more loving within ourselves and to those who live with us, they take that love out into the world and it spreads. So much aggression in the world is caused by the absence of love in one's life.

I encourage you to practice being more loving to those around you and observe how things begin to shift.

When Even a Shower Won't Take That Feeling Away

"I am no bird; and no net ensnares me: I am a free human being with an independent will." — Charlotte Brontë, *Author*

Do you currently, or have you ever had, someone in your life who causes you to feel anxious, irritated, upset or angry? Even after this person leaves, or you hang up the phone, do you find yourself feeling a kind of film on your body that even a shower can't take away? We all have people like this in our lives and although we want to love everyone it doesn't mean that we cannot choose to set healthy boundaries – in essence cherry-picking within our lives and releasing any unhealthy, toxic relationships.

Judy was a well-intentioned, hardworking mother of two; a marathon runner and devoted wife. She worked in a hospital lab, primarily surrounded by other women. Judy found that there was a great deal of gossip, much of it hurtful. In addition, she also found that one woman in particular was being exceptionally catty. Judy became uncomfortable and even chose to work the night shift in order to avoid this woman even though it affected her health and her family.

Judy tried to remain positive but the stress of work was wearing her down. She thought about looking for another job but that would mean an extra-long commute, as the closest hospitals were about sixty miles away. Judy was my running partner and I suggested she be a catalyst for change and that perhaps what everyone needed was for someone to take a stand and recreate a more positive environment. The first thing she would need to do was start with herself, take responsibility and release the three J's.

Over time Judy, who was in a management position, implemented a "positive attitude only" rule. She suggested that staff members not complain and instead, if they had a challenge, to come to her with solutions and ideas for how they might be able to shift the situation. Eventually the people who were the most negative transformed before Judy's eyes and the woman who had been the key instigator left for another job.

What Judy did was change the rules. First she stopped complaining about her situation. Next she created boundaries letting people know that negativity would not be tolerated around her. Thirdly, she journaled her feelings and expressed any frustrations in private written words. She became much happier, healthier and released so much stress that people commented that she even looked younger.

In our lives there will always be people with whom we do not share the same views, values or opinions. We have a choice: we can either choose to live with it and love them anyway, or we can create boundaries and let people know what we are willing and not willing to tolerate. If you have a girlfriend who gossips all of the time let her know that you do not want to have those conversations. If you know someone who complains about everything, tell her that you are open to helping her find solutions but complaining only serves to make both of you feel bad.

People will come in and out of our lives. If someone is causing you to feel bad it is not your responsibility to change them; we can only ever change ourselves and create clear-cut boundaries. If someone is not willing to stop gossiping or stop being so negative they will most likely stop speaking to you and may eventually drop out of your life. If you have negative family members, from experience I can tell you that as you lay the ground rules they will eventually stop that form of behavior in front of you. They may not do it in the rest of their lives however in your presence, it will stop.

Make a decision to set boundaries with people. Your time is valuable. At the end of the day, you will not look back and wish you had gossiped more or spent more valuable time with someone who was complaining; instead you will wish you spent more time with the people who were positive and uplifting. You may have to have some tough conversations, but they will be worth it. Like Judy, by creating a clearing in your life, you will feel better about yourself and you will find the world a much better place.

Putting Your Family First

"I feel my family's needs are a priority. I'm not comfortable with the idea of serving the many and ignoring my family."

— Susan Sarandon, *Actress*

The great Green Bay Packers football coach, Vince Lombardi, said the same thing to his players every year: "Your priorities are this, and in this order – God, your family and football." Lombardi led his team to five national championships in seven years.

What Lombardi understood was that when a person's priorities were built in a solid foundation there was nothing that could not be accomplished. What was true for Green Bay's success is also true in our lives; when our family is in harmony, we feel more productive, happier and more fulfilled. Putting our family first doesn't necessarily imply that we focus there in spite of all else; what it means is that we make a daily effort to invest in our families so that we maintain healthy balance.

As women, it can be seductive to spend more time at work, sit on boards, do charity work, and attend functions or events only to have your family come second. Children are precious and they are only young for so long. Among the thousands of women that I have worked with, the number-one issue when it comes to family is guilt. As women we tend to feel guilty when we are working and not with our children; likewise we feel guilty being with our children and having other things pile up.

I was once a workaholic, putting in long days. I went to work before my daughter got up and often returned after she was in bed. She spent more time with a caregiver than she did with me. I told myself that this was for the good of the family; however, I could see that our relationship was strained. This was a catalyst for going into business for myself. I did not see how I could ever experience a fulfilling relationship with my child while working eighty-hour weeks.

Many women I know struggle with this. We call it the work-life balance paradigm. Essentially, we are expected to produce on par with men, take salaries that are still on average about thirty percent lower than a man's, and somehow manage to not have children raised by a nanny. This is taking a toll on women, with the average working mother feeling extremely overwhelmed, guilty, anxious and turning to alcohol and antidepressants as coping mechanisms.

This was the impetus for Anne-Marie Slaughter's article in the Atlantic, appropriately entitled, "Why Women Still Can't *Have It All*." As women we want to feel that we are doing meaningful work, we want loving relationships and we also want a degree of freedom. Can we *have it all* if we are a slave to the whimsy of the modern-day work expectations of fifty-plus-hour weeks and 24/7 on-demand texting and calls?

I would argue that yes, we can *have it all*, even if we have demanding careers. Will we need to set boundaries? Yes. Will we need to ensure that we dedicate time to do meaningful things with our families? Yes. Will we sometimes need to say the word "no"? Yes. Will we need to find creative solutions? Yes. Will we perhaps need to find a new job with more flexible hours, child care options and understanding employers who value the family? Yes. Will it necessarily be easy? No.

There are options out there if you are willing to look. More and more companies are offering women the opportunity to work from home one or more days per week, have flexible hours or job share. If, like me, you find that you want to stop going to work, there are other support systems for starting your own business, including financing. Network marketing has provided many women with full-time incomes while they work from home. This was my preferred method in leaving the workforce and it has been my goal to liberate families through this business model.

Regardless of what is happening for you career-wise right now, it is imperative that you do put your family first. A study done by the National Center for Addiction and Substance Abuse, at Columbia University, found that children who sat down for dinner with their families 5-7 times per week were four times less likely to have substance abuse problems. A study published in October 2010 by the Montreal-based think tank CIRANO found that children who were put into early daycare were later to read, write and experienced poor communication skills. Almost 69% of mothers with children under two are back in the workforce.

While work is often a necessity with financial demands, it is in no way an excuse to put our families on the back burner. Creative solutions such as video Skyping into meal times, leaving little notes in a child's lunch, sending romantic texts to our partners, or negotiating with the boss to go in earlier so you can leave earlier may be required. Ultimately, whatever we neglect will eventually demand our attention. If we neglect our family we may soon have to put everything else on hold to deal with addictions, challenging behavior and so forth.

It took a few years to change my life; however, the process was rewarding and although it was tough at times, I do not regret a minute. While I was transitioning out of work, I began building my network marketing business. I would put the kids to bed and spend two hours, four nights per week, making calls and connecting with people. After ten months I was able to leave my job because I had created a six-figure income.

While I was juggling multiple balls in the air, I had a conversation with my boss and asked for flexibility. I wanted to be able to take my daughter to school and also pick her up. I also wanted for my son to not have to be in daycare five days per week. I proposed a solution in that I would make myself available for a certain number of hours per week, which included some evenings as I was expected to attend business dinners, and in return I could be flexible as long as I did the work.

Today my life is totally different. In my current work day I start at ten o'clock a.m. and work until four o'clock. Between four o'clock and eight-thirty o'clock it is family time. I put down all technology and instead the focus is on homework, getting kids to lessons and also sitting down for dinner as a family. Chris and children know that no one, at this time, is more important than they are.

If I do need to schedule something I ask permission. Because this doesn't happen very often, my family is very open when such situations arise. Having grown up in a single-parent family, I made a decision that it was vital to put my family first. I love what we have created. Family was the number-one reason I decided to become a full-time entrepreneur where I could choose my own hours and get paid what I deserved.

Your children and your partner, if you have one, need to know that they are special to you. If your life is chaotic and out of balance then make some changes right now. Sit down as a family and decide to get on track. Commit to having meals together as often as possible; take time to connect as a family and share daily "high points;" make an effort to be present at big sporting events, recitals and other school functions; and most importantly, know that although the work to shift things around might feel onerous, it will ultimately be worth it.

Once Bitten

"You never lose by loving. You always lose by holding back."

— Barbara Deangelis, *Author*

After my former husband and I parted, I was emotionally bankrupt, stricken with MS, and financially devastated. I left for Toronto and lived on my brother-in-law's sofa for about a month. After a couple of paychecks and attracting a great apartment only steps away from my job, I was able to live on my own. This was the first time in over ten years that I had lived by myself. It was exhilarating and terrifying at the same time.

In the daytime I went to the health club, where my office was based, and spent much of my free time training for the triathlon. I kept myself busy so I wouldn't be depressed. My grandmother had always professed that work was indeed therapy, and I threw myself into mine. I also went into "anti-man" mode. I cut off all my long hair, went without make-up and became androgynous. I was just too broken and too hurt to contemplate being in a relationship.

I watched the other women I worked with either go on dates or make plans with their boyfriends. For me, Friday night meant working or staying in. During this time I read books on healing, the law of attraction and made a conscious decision that if I had inadvertently attracted my former life I could absolutely be the creator of my future life.

One of my favorite aunts, Gloria, was also single at the time and living in the same city. I would call her up and chat about men. Together we conspired about what the ideal man would look like. Together we decided to make a list.

Initially my list included 54 items. It didn't take me long to realize that 54 items might be a little extreme. I mean, honestly, those are some big expectations. I also wasn't creating a clearing for any man to actually grow with me; I was looking for the ideal man to simply walk into my life, and that wasn't a fair expectation either.

The list then shortened to ten things that were an absolute must; these were my non-negotiables. I would not compromise and I would not be denied. This list became my gold standard. Everywhere I went I looked at men and wondered which one of them had the exact qualities I was seeking in a life partner. I had done it wrong once before and was not about to do it again.

This was my list:

1. I want a man who loves me completely for who I am as a person.

2. I want a man who loves my daughter as his own.
3. I want a man who has faith in God.
4. I want a man who honors his health and likes to exercise.
5. I want a man who has a sense of adventure.
6. I want a man who loves to travel.
7. I want a man who is monogamous and committed.
8. I want a man who will be my partner.
9. I want a man who is willing to grow and is open.
10. I want a man who makes me feel safe and loved.

After writing this list, I carried it with me everywhere. In the meantime I worked on me; I had to be the woman worthy of a man who had these qualities and I also had to create space for him in my life. Even though I had the "scarlet letter" in many ways – having MS, being divorced, a single mom and also struggling financially – I knew that I also had a lot to give and so I also left part of my closet with empty hangers and cleared a spot in my bathroom drawer for "his" things, whoever "he" was.

One evening I was watching the sunset from my fifteenth-floor apartment in midtown Toronto. The sky was full of brilliant beams of crimson, scarlet, magenta and fiery orange. This was the kind of sunset that you just wished would go on for hours.

I looked across the skyline towards the other buildings. I set my focus on the tallest one within my sight. I asked myself who would live there? What was going on in their lives? Were they in pain like I was? Were they full of hope like I also was? What were their dreams and goals?

I had a vase of roses which were fading on my balcony. The roses had been marked down to $3.00 for me. They had been perfect and I think the woman who ran the vegetable stand I patronized felt that I could use them. I picked up a wilting rose and began throwing petals over the balcony as the sun continued to set. I recited my list.

The next day I went to work after an early swim practice. My hair was its usual wavy, unruly mess. I was wearing yoga pants and an oversize sweatshirt. One of my staff had called in sick and I was stocking the towels.

I looked up and caught sight of a man who seemed very familiar. In fact, I was certain that it was a guy I had gone to high school with in Brockville, the small town I had grown up in. This wasn't any ordinary guy – it was Chris Arkeveld, the boy who every girl had wanted to date.

When I was in high school I was the typical hormone-ravaged girl. I fell in love with Chris Arkeveld the moment I saw him when I was in grade nine and he was in grade twelve. I would see Chris in the halls and go weak in the knees. He was blonde-haired, blue-eyed perfection and I was the ugly duckling – the half-Chinese, darker-skinned, pimple-faced girl and definitely not a girl he would have ever noticed.

Of course, I felt he was out of my league back then, and I could only love him from afar. I decided, being the young salesperson I was then, to trade lockers with people so I could get close to him. I never spoke to him but would occasionally try to say hello if I could get past the nerve-induced nausea.

I did get up the courage to ask him to dance one night. We did dance, to one slow song, when I was in grade ten. I am sure he did it out of pity more than anything though he maintains today that he thought I was "cute."

When we finished university he wanted to ask me out, but I was dating the man who would be my first husband, so nothing came of it. I would see him in passing and my heart would flutter a bit. Because I was already with someone I wasn't open to anything.

Here we were, many years later in Toronto, with Chris walking into my club and me looking like a train wreck. I went to the front desk computer after he swiped his membership card. I needed to verify that it was indeed Chris Arkeveld. Not only did I confirm that it was Chris; his membership status said, "single."

I went to the change room to apply some mascara and see what I could do with my hair. I didn't have any other clothes at work so I had to make do with what I had available. After getting myself into as decent of an appearance as I possibly could, given the circumstances, I headed out to find him.

So many thoughts were going through my mind. What if he thought I was fat? At that time I was thirty pounds more than I was in high school and also more than my current weight. My adrenals had been so shot that I had gained thirty pounds in record time. What if he didn't remember me? What if he was a jerk?

I decided to silence my chattering mind and simply go have a conversation. He was lifting weights and looking really, really fine. I went up to him and asked, "Are you Chris Arkeveld?" Great opener, I know. However, it was the best I could think of.

He said that he was and I asked him if he remembered me. He had that blank look of "I don't know who the heck you are" on his face. Nevertheless, he was very polite until we pursued the conversation further and something clicked. We had gone to a small high school but it wasn't as though he had been my best friend or anything like that.

He asked me if I would like to get a drink sometime. I said that it would be lovely. I gave him my card and attempted to be casual about it. I wondered if he could see my heart pumping under my oversized sweatshirt.

I waited for him to call. I had been out of dating for so long that I didn't know what the rules were. Do I call him? Does he call me? What should I do?

I phoned a girlfriend who worked in the publishing industry and asked her what the new standard was. She had gone to high school with both Chris and myself and suggested that a guy like him was a bit more traditional and that I should wait. She also said that he likely wasn't calling because my last name was now different.

I took my friend's sage words to heart and decided to up the stakes. I had our entire front desk team on Chris alert. They were to call me when he came into the club. I also took other measures. I started wearing some make-up every day – just enough to look awake. I also began taking steps to getting healthy and as a result dropped seven pounds quickly.

About a week and a half later (it actually seemed like ten years) I got a call from Suzy at the front desk. He was here. Heart pounding, I gave him ten minutes to get changed and then hunted him down. With my stomach in my throat, I asked him if he was going to call me for that drink or what. He said, "How about this Thursday?" I was elated.

On our first date we didn't kiss. We just talked. Chris had broken up with his girlfriend months prior. We were both single, alone, and forging ahead with our careers. He walked me home and I prayed to God that I would see him again. I knew that night that Chris had everything on my list.

The next Monday we had our second date and have been together ever since. Our life together has been incredible. We have had our ups and downs. We have had arguments. We haven't always seen eye-to-eye, but we love one another and are in love. We have grown together and that growth has not always been easy. In our house we are committed and divorce is not an option.

In the beginning of our relationship we struggled with trust. Chris and I had both come out of painful relationships that had left us not fully able to fully surrender to one another. Having both been betrayed in the past, we were slightly broken. It took several years to fully become T.U.A. with each other. Through that growth and through the pain that comes with reframing one's beliefs we have become best friends.

In 2012, we travelled to Bali as a family to recommit our wedding vows. We had a ceremony overlooking the ocean as the sun set over the Pacific. Looking into my husband's eyes after such history together, I was more in love with him than I had been during our first wedding. The years of overcoming challenges and giving up our egos have taught us to be partners first and foremost.

If you have been once bitten it does not mean you should be twice shy. You can attract the ideal partner, but the first and foremost step is to become the person you would want to be in a relationship with. If you have attracted one or more relationships that have ended in pain and heartbreak, then take some time to focus on yourself; live into the life pyramid, create a solid foundation in health, faith and self-love and then you will be ready to focus forward, attracting the person who will be your lover, your best friend and the very person who completes your soul.

It's Never Too Late to Ignite Your Relationship or Find Passion

"An archeologist is the best husband any woman can have; the older she gets, the more interested he is in her." —Agatha Christie, *Author*

"My wife and I haven't had sex in five years," our friend confessed to us after we polished off a very nice Barolo. Chris and I were in shock. Five years! As parents with young children, we may not be as amorous as those who are newly in relationships, but we do put the effort in. By "effort" I mean that yes, sometimes it does take an extra bit of drive to overcome the fatigue that comes with parenting, hormone imbalance or the non-stop "to –do" list in our heads; however, once the sex stops, can the relationship still exist?

I didn't think my friend was having an affair, though who really knows. A June 2012 article on Fox News Online suggested that almost seventy percent of men cheat on their wives and up to sixty percent of women cheat on their husbands. The number-one cause is lack of interest. As someone who has experienced infidelity, I can relate to how painful it is. When I went through it I felt numb. I was so angry. I felt violated. I also questioned what I had done to attract that experience into my life.

Taking responsibility in a relationship isn't always easy. When we want more than the person is willing to give – in the case of my friend and his wife it was that, according to him, she didn't want to have sex – then only the most saintly, dedicated people are willing to go for long periods of time feeling unfulfilled. Ultimately it is not just about sex, it is about how we are in love, and sometimes the way we operate doesn't work with the other person's desires.

Psychologist Dr. Gary Chapman has done a tremendous amount of research on the subject. His book, The Five Love Languages, is a worldwide bestseller. Dr. Chapman asserts that there are five separate ways in which people prefer to have love expressed. These range from physical touch, to words of affirmation, to gifts, to gestures and acts of service. Dr. Chapman maintains that if we do not experience love from another in a way that we deem meaningful, then this is where the problems arise.

Knowing your love language and your partner's love language is helpful. If you are showering your partner with gifts when all he truly appreciates is physical touch then you are not going keep the passion going. By the same token, if your love language is being acknowledged by words of appreciation and your partner tries to express his love by fondling your breasts then you will soon feel violated. Ultimately, in any passionate relationship there is going to be some give and take and that is what keeps it interesting.

The next secret to igniting passion is to stop comparing what you have to the past. The moment you let go of the "if only" and move into possibility, you shift your reality. Stop focusing on the past and what was. It prevents you from creating something even more vibrant in the future. Passion requires creativity; how will you ever be innovative in your love life if you relive the past?

My husband was lamenting, one day, about how passionate we were when we first started dating. Of course, we didn't have four children and a full life. I shared with him that by focusing on the past it was closing the door to what could be in the future. Passion changes and love intensifies the longer we are with someone. By the same token, people who live only for the passion find themselves disappointed when it comes to long-term commitment.

I am always looking for creative ways to experience greater connection with my husband. Having four children doesn't always provide opportunities to indulge in solitary time. Sometimes I write him a random email detailing ten things I love about him at that moment or leave a little Post-It note for him with an invitation for a kiss or something more. I also know that when I take care of and love myself, Chris is more appreciative. If I am self-deprecating it is a major turn-off. No one wants to hear their partner putting themselves down.

A few suggestions for keeping the sparks alive:

- Schedule a set date night—you can stay in, go out...Either way, make the time.
- Leave a random love note or card of appreciation.
- Take a class together.
- Schedule a romantic night away.

- Play "dress up" for your partner.
- Write a list of ten things you appreciate about your partner and leave it on the pillow.
- Book a "you choose" afternoon and allow your partner to choose an activity—ladies, you are fairly certain what will be chosen. Just go with it.
- Watch a movie, sporting event or something your partner wants to watch.
- Buy concert tickets to your partner's favorite artist.
- Leave a "randy" note in your partner's computer bag or wallet.
- Lastly—ease up, girlfriend—as women we can get really uptight.

Why Women Need Other Women

"But really, we also need to learn how to love one another as women. How to appreciate and respect each other." — Chaka Khan, *Musician*

Think of the great female friendships of our time. Oprah Winfrey and Gayle King, Courtney Cox and Jennifer Aniston are two celebrity examples of dedicated friendships. In fiction, think of the gals from Sex in the City; didn't you want to be part of that dynamic foursome? These girls could laugh and cry together and not skip one designer beat in their Manolos.

In my twenties and early thirties, I didn't think women needed to have female friends. I thought that I was doing just fine with having some close male friends. It was at a seminar with Dr. John Gray, author of Men are from Mars, Women are from Venus, that it clicked for me. Not only did I need some close female friends; I had to first develop friendships with women, because up to that point I hadn't let any of them into my life.

Dr. Gray shares that when women talk about whatever is going on in our lives it raises serotonin, a neuro-chemical that creates a "feel-good" sensation. When we hold our problems in, they can fester and can cause sadness, anger and frustration.

For men, talking about their problems can cause a drop in dopamine, the male "feel-good" neuro-chemical. This is also why your man may tune out when you talk about purse shopping; he simply cannot relate.

Dr. Gray also says that women need other women as companions. It can even help our relationships with our partners. When we have a place to vent, be silly, conspire, chat and express ourselves we feel better. When we feel better we are more loving. When we are more loving we set the stage for experiencing an even more fulfilling and sensual love. You get the idea.

We need other women in our lives – women who are special or extraordinary. Perhaps you have a woman friend or even a female family member who you can trust and have fun with. Maybe this is not the case. A great place to meet other like-minded women is at seminars, women's networking groups, exercise classes, spirituality centers, churches and clubs. You will find that there are great women out there if you would start seeking.

Often there are women we know casually but we do not yet have a close relationship with. They may be women admire from afar because they are funny, sociable, well-intentioned or just downright awesome. These women could become great friends if you would take the time to truly get to know them. Just like in dating, it is your responsibility to make the first move. Always bear in mind, however, that establishing trust is essential to all relationships.

Collaborating with Men

"Creativity comes from a conflict of ideas." — Donatella Versace, *Designer*

When it comes to men and women, as John Gray says, men often seem as though they really are from Mars. Just pick up any magazine for men and the focus is how to get six-pack abs and be a winner in the bedroom. I think they throw other articles in just to create the illusion of substance. The reality is that men make life more interesting and great collaborations can often come when the brain of a woman and a man unite.

One of the most powerful women on the planet is Oprah Winfrey. She is an example of a strong, independent woman who is able to collaborate and even evolve the careers of men such as Dr. Phil and Dr. Oz. Oprah does not appear to be threatened by men, nor does she appear to want to be one; instead Oprah has seemingly mastered the art of collaboration with the opposite gender, which has yielded some beautiful outcomes.

As women, especially if we have experienced abuse in our past, the idea of collaborating with a man can feel intimidating. Often our old hurts, pains and stories are carried into our career and these can be transferred onto our colleagues, business partners and every professional relationship we have with a man. If we allow our past hurts to get in the way of collaborations with the opposite gender we are likely miss out on extremely rich opportunities.

Some of my best friends and business colleagues are men. Many of my greatest business mentors have also been men. Men offer a unique perspective in their ability to focus on a singular task, not get overly caught up with office politics or gossip and think linearly. As women we can operate more from the realm of the emotional rather than the rational and even be our own worst enemies in our own work or business environment.

I have worked in male-dominated offices. It can be a lot of fun. I have participated in hockey pools, poker games and chatting about who won football over the weekend. Getting to know the guys and speaking their language can help you win some allies, as long as you maintain your stance as a woman. Even though many men are not looking for sexual encounters in the workplace, be sure to send the message that you are professional and friendly to avoid any confusion.

Ask yourself what you can learn from the men around you. Take time to observe their habits, attitudes and work. Ask yourself if there is anything you admire or can emulate from the successful men you know. Finally, seek to collaborate with successful men and other women, as it is said that the five people you spend the most time with will either elevate or demote your own level of success.

Learning from Our Relationship History

"I have found the paradox that if I love until it hurts, then there is no hurt, but only more love." — Mother Teresa

Our first relationships begin the moment we are born. From infancy we are learning cause and effect. Often when an infant cries someone picks her up. That infant is taught that crying yields a response. In some cases a crying infant is not picked up and so the infant learns that crying is useless.

As children we delve into more complex relationships. We learn cause and effect with our friends, family and authority figures. Children from the same home can grow to become different people not only because they are different genetically but also because their relationships with people outside the home are different. Our relationships in childhood form how we react and respond in adulthood.

In coaching clients over the years, we have often identified one childhood memory that shaped an adult belief. This memory is not always painful or necessarily significant, but sometimes, the most innocuous event can shape our future.

When I was in grade nine I had a best friend, Megan. She and I were both runners and in the same grade. She was blonde, blue-eyed and gorgeous. She came from a two-parent family that also included an older, also-gorgeous sister. I, on the other hand, was dark-haired, with brown eyes, from a single-parent home. I always compared myself to Megan and wished that my life could be like hers.

One day we were at my house doing homework. It was the day before a big track meet. Megan and I were running against one another. My dad innocently asked Megan if she was going to win the race. I was stunned, shocked, sad, angry and humiliated all at once on account of my father's question. Megan, ever the lady, replied, "One of us will, either Sue or myself." The next day, sure enough, Megan and I raced. She won and I came second. I felt so defeated. My dad was there and congratulated me, but it felt empty.

From that day forward I always felt second best. I didn't try to win races because I knew, in my dad's eyes, that I wasn't a winner. I continued to be second best in my class, second choice for boys and just plain second all over the map. My relationship with my dad also changed. I felt unloved and unappreciated.

This one incident translated into sabotage later in life. I didn't go into races to try to win; I went in to come in the top three. It was getting ridiculous. I knew I had the talent to win but I did not believe I could.

Several years later I had a "clearing conversation" with my father. A clearing conversation is one where two people essentially release anything that they are feeling without an attachment to the outcome. I felt that I had to clear that with my dad. My father was shocked that I remembered and confessed feeling bad at that time. He had completely forgotten that Megan and I would be in the same race because I usually did not race the 3000 meters.

I had spent years coming second because I thought I would never be first in my dad's eyes. I had spent years settling for anything but first place. One incident had affected many relationships, especially how I interacted with my father or men with similar characteristics. I realized that it only takes one incident, one misinterpretation, or one event to change the course of your life.

Regardless of where you are right now, reflecting on your childhood can provide some valuable insights into your present relationships. Perhaps you are holding onto a memory and have created a false perception from that event, much like I did. The only way to move forward is to change our belief through changing our perception of the event. This requires taking responsibility and additionally releasing the excuses that have been brewing throughout our lives.

Changing our beliefs requires strength. Maya Angelou says, "Without courage you cannot practice any of the other virtues." I encourage you to consider that you are not a victim of your past relationships. Perhaps you have created false beliefs and by releasing these you can unlock your ability to have richer relationships with everyone in your life.

In the next segment, we will focus on healing our hearts through reflection and gratitude. This exercise has brought peace to many women and it is something I have used many times myself to release my false perceptions and transform my beliefs.

Healing Our Hearts—The Gratitude Process

"Forgiveness is a gift you give yourself."

— Suzanne Somers, *Actress and Author*

One of the things I have taught over the years is how to make peace with difficult people in our lives. Not only do we have toxins in our bodies; we can also have them in our minds. Ultimately, these "mind toxins" affect our current relationships and the partnerships we are looking to create.

In Dr. John Demartini's landmark book, The Breakthrough Experience, he teaches people how to "collapse" people who are not serving them. Dr. Demartini says that all people have something to teach us. When we sit in a place of resentment, guilt, frustration or hatred we will be held back in our life. He shares that even the seemingly most evil people have gifts to give.

To better understand how to shift our beliefs and heal our wounds, we must embrace the knowledge that every person and every situation has a gift to give us if we are open to receiving it, as we discussed earlier in this chapter. Until we understand what this gift is, we will repeat our patterns of attracting this type of person without benefiting from the relationship.

Many books urge us to forgive, although forgiveness without true gratitude is not enough. Forgiveness is incredible when it truly comes from the heart. To look at the most challenging person or situation in our lives, and be grateful for that individual or that event, sends us to a place that is much more powerful that simply uttering the words, "I'm sorry." Gratitude takes us to a place of peace. When we are at peace we can love more deeply and attract more desirable people and events to ourselves.

You may be thinking, "Susan, this person really hurt me. How can I be grateful for them?" The answer is to simply think as God thinks: with pure unconditional love. When we are grateful for those who have hurt us, we see these people through the lens of God's eyes.

In order to fully go through the process, we must first identify the person or situation that is causing us pain. The steps are done in sequence and are powerful. At the end of this chapter, the empowerment exercise is to follow The Gratitude Process and release our limiting beliefs around one or more people. By doing this, you will truly be set free. Your relationships will become more vibrant and you will experience greater peace than you may have ever known.

The gratitude process contains ten key steps:

1. Identify a situation or person who caused you pain.
2. What were/are the characteristics of the person/situation?
3. Does or did anyone else in your life have these characteristics?
4. If yes, who are they?
5. How am I a better person for experiencing this event/knowing this person?
6. What is great about this?
7. What are/were the lessons I learned from this about myself?
8. Am I willing to fully let it go?
9. What am I grateful for?
10. Write a letter to the person in the situation or to yourself.

One of the people I used this process on was my mother. To even write about her with peace took me many, many years. When I finally realized that she had given me a tremendous gift I felt true love toward her for the first time in my life. From there I was able to love her fully and have T.U.A. My mother is my mother. I love her fully and am grateful for all of the experiences I have had with her in my life.

The incident I worked on releasing was the fact that my mother left me alone at such a young age. For years I attracted the wrong men just so I wouldn't be alone. I was petrified of the dark and I was frightened of being abandoned. Releasing my mother allowed me to attract my great love, Chris, and our relationship has been, and continues to be, amazing.

This is an example of how I used this process on my mother:

1. Identify a situation or person who caused you pain.
   · My mother leaving me alone.

2. What were/are the characteristics of the person/situation?
   · Aloof · Addict · Victim · Saboteur · Liar

3. Does or did anyone else in your life have these characteristics?
   · Yes

4. Who are they?
   · Bob · Jim

5. How am I a better person for knowing him/her?
   · I am a great mother. I make sure my children always feel safe. They know Chris and I are there for them.

6. What is great about this?
   · I am so grateful to my mother because her neglect helped me become very conscientious as a parent.

7. What are/were the lessons learnt about myself?
   · I am resilient. I am a survivor.

8. Am I willing to fully let it go?
   · Yes

9. What am I grateful for?
   · I am so grateful to my mother. I do know that she wanted the best for me. Her way of teaching me was to illustrate how not to be and I love her for it. I am the woman I am today because of her.

The tenth step is to write a letter to yourself as if you are still in the situation or to the person who affected you. The letter must be one of gratitude and also a sharing of the pain it may have caused you. If you are writing to yourself in the past then write to yourself at the age you were when the event occurred.

We have helped so many people in the gratitude process. Women have freed themselves of bullies, let go of toxic people, become better mothers, wives, partners and friends. I continue to use the ten steps whenever something comes up that I do not feel great about. This process can help you become a *have it all woman*.

A Last Thought on Relationships

"After all, computers crash, people die, relationships fall apart. The best we can do is breathe and reboot." — Sarah Jessica Parker, *Actress*

In all relationships it is important to remember that people will come and go from our lives. The friends who saw you through one season may not be there for the next. As we grow and see the world through new eyes we also see how some relationships no longer serve us. If we are in a place of aiming to be positive then the negative people in our lives only serve to reinforce the notion of who we no longer wish to be.

If a relationship isn't serving us or is abusive or harmful, then we have to let it go and move on. Our life is too short to be with people who do not want the very best for us, although in the realm of marriage and commitment we may have to work hard to get that relationship to where we want it to be. You may have people in your life, or even your partner, who really do deserve to be in your life – invest in those relationships and do not be afraid to let the others go.

Ultimately all relationships mirror back to us our feelings about who we truly are. As we shift our beliefs, choose to let go of jealousy, judgment and justification, invest in our primary relationships, collaborate with other women and men and release our past hurts using the Gratitude Process, we create *have it all* relationships, living a beautiful, rich and fulfilling life.

Use the Four-D Principle for Fulfilling Relationships

Decide to see the gift in everyone.

Define your inner and outer circle.

Delete the Three J's.

Definitive Action: Gratitude process, T.U.A. list, invest in primary relationships.

Have It All Affirmation

I attract beautiful, fulfilling relationships and partnerships in all areas of my life. I choose to see the gift in everyone and people see the gifts in me.

- *HAVE IT ALL WOMAN* EMPOWERMENT EXERCISE -

The Gratitude Process

Is there a person or people in your life with whom you have relationships that need to be healed? Take time and go through the Gratitude Process. Work through the ten steps. It may be quite painful or it may require very little effort. Mastering this process is one of the steps required to becoming a *have it all woman*. Answer the following questions and then take time to finish with a letter to that person, even if they are no longer living, and read it aloud. This is an extremely powerful process—one that can truly provide peace to your soul.

1. *Identify a situation or person who caused you pain.*
2. *What were/are the characteristics of the person/situation?*
3. *Does/did anyone else in your life have these characteristics?*
4. *If yes, who are they?*
5. *How am I a better person for experiencing this event/knowing this person?*
6. *What is great about this?*
7. *What were the lessons I learned from this about myself?*
8. *Am I willing to fully let it go?*
9. *What am I grateful for?*

Write a letter to the person or to yourself as if you are still in the situation.

CHAPTER SEVEN

Step 7: Creating Financial Ease

"Everything in life ... has to have balance."

— Donna Karan, *Designer and Entrepreneur*

CHAPTER SEVEN

Step 7: Creating Financial Ease

From Laid Off to Well Off

"In all circumstances, I always look for the light and build around it, with little memory of pain." — Diane Von Furstenberg, *Designer*

Sandra Wilson was a frustrated mom. In 1994, after finishing her maternity leave, she found out that she would be laid off from her job at Canadian Airlines. Sandra was madly in love with her new son, Robbie, and the thought of putting him in daycare broke her heart. Dealing with her frustration, Sandra decided to creatively solve another issue: finding shoes that would stay on Robbie's feet.

Concocting a pair of shoes from an old leather purse, Sandra created a crossover slipper/shoe that remained in place while Robbie kicked and played. From there, the ideas continued to flow and as friends saw the shoes the demand began; a business was born.

In a quote from the Government of Canada's website, Sandra shares, "Running my own business was quite a major learning curve," she says. The first few years were a crash course in manufacturing, sourcing suppliers, distribution, packaging, marketing, sales and financing. "I knew nothing about this business. I'd never worked in retail; I'd never worked in wholesale. I didn't know how to manufacture; I didn't even know what should go in the box when you ship an order. I learned it all on the job. It was very challenging."

That same year, Sandra made thirty pairs of the little shoes she called Robeez. She took them to the Vancouver Gift Show. From there she received fifteen retail accounts and now she was faced with additional challenges, including how to meet demand and produce a high-quality product in alignment with her brand. She was able to grow the business to a certain point but knew she needed help. She brought in salespeople, hired consultants, and as the business expanded into more markets, her staff grew to forty-five people.

By 2006, what started as a home-based business in her basement was now a fledgling empire with five hundred staff and market share in Canada, the United States, Australia, the U.K. and more. Sandra Wilson sold her twelve-year-old business for almost thirty million dollars to Stride Rite ™, a U.S.-based shoe maker, and continued to give creative input on the brand.

Out of the forced need to create more income and the desire to solve a problem, Sandra Wilson went from laid-off to quite well off. It did not happen overnight and there was a great deal of learning along the way. She was not a seamstress, nor did she have a background in manufacturing. What Sandra Wilson was, was a woman on a mission with a desire to improve the circumstances of her family. Her courage, drive and determination is a message to women everywhere that with the willingness to work, focus for years, learn and grow – anyone can change their circumstances.

Money Matters

"A big part of financial freedom is having your heart and mind free from worry about the what-ifs of life."

— Suze Orman, T*elevision Personality and Money Expert*

It is said that money is not important until it becomes important. In other words, money isn't relevant until there is a pressing need; money matters. Life is full of unexpected demands, from a health crisis to a lay-off to a home repair; there will always be times when we require money just to get through. The sad truth is that many women do not have control of their money; the average woman is shouldering credit card debt, lines of credit, supporting her family and saving very little. Statistics illustrate that when it comes to money, unfortunately the likelihood is that the average woman is not as financially savvy as she should be.

In the United States it is estimated that the average person retires with approximately $2500 in the bank. They rely on social security to subsidize them. With the financial crisis that befell the world in 2008, many people lost a large portion of any savings that were invested in the stock market and additionally many also lost their jobs. Those that did remain in the work force were saddled with other financial burdens, including a large influx of adult children returning home to live with their parents because of the high unemployment rate for generation Y.

In the 1970s, seventy percent of women stayed home to raise children. In today's economy, over seventy percent of women work away from the home. For some women it is by choice, while for the vast majority it is by necessity. Yes, we have become our own worst enemies because of our choices to be ravenous consumers. The average middle-class woman lives in a fairly sizable home, has two vehicles, eats at restaurants and carries at least one designer handbag. Her predecessor from the 1970s had one vehicle, tended to eat at home more often, lived in a more modest home and the need to have designer goods was relegated to the rich. It is a different world.

As we live into a *have it all* life, it is imperative to understand that struggle is not part of the equation. We have spent time working on health, faith, self-love and relationships, building a solid foundation for financial ease. To create this ease there are only two choices – spend less or make more. Either way, it begins with understanding your money, taking responsibility and deciding how much you need to "invite the easy" into your life.

I have struggled with money and I have made ample money. I have been bankrupt and I have been a millionaire. The thing I will tell you, wholeheartedly, is that there is no glamour in struggle. Having money to deal with emergencies, take family vacations, pay the bills on time, save for children's college educations, give to charities that mean something to us, buy gifts for loved ones, and – yes girls, purchase the occasional handbag, is much better than living paycheck to paycheck.

From experience, I know it is possible to change any situation. Within three years I went from living on my brother-in-law's sofa to starting the business that made me millions. There will always be a period of challenge as we work to shift our circumstances and we have to be willing to do that work, deal with the criticism of others and stay true to our dreams. The biggest thing to understand is that no matter where you are at right now – you can change your life.

In this book we have profiled great women like Dr. Iyanla Vanzant, who went from a woman on welfare to a lawyer, author and television personality; Liz Murray, who went from homeless to Harvard; and Sandra Wilson, a laid-off mom to multi-millionaire. Do these women have anything you don't? Of course not. They simply understand that yes, money does matter, and if you pursue your dreams, take a stand in your own life and commit to changing your circumstances – anything is possible.

Where You Are Right Now is Dictated By Your Past

"Everyone can get a little sloppy with cash and it's smart to notice. But what's squeezing you is the big stuff you ladle onto your credit cards."

—Jane Bryant, *Journalist*

To understand the present, we must look at the past. All of our current money situations are a result of something we have learned. Financially, we are a culmination of the habits we have created due to these money lessons. We may have the habit of spending what we do not have because that is what our parents did, and now we are in debt. Or, we may be very budget-conscious and due to the habit of saving, are in a place of abundance. Either way, our habits are rooted in our childhood.

Let's start with your upbringing. As children we observe what our parents did and created our own "story" around the interpretation. All it takes is witnessing one argument over money and our perception is changed forever. The point at which we visit the places in our past where our money story was created, it is to that degree we can unglue the fabric of our current situation.

My earliest memories of money started when I was quite young. My parents divorced when I was three, and leading up to the separation they fought. At night I would hide under my bed as they yelled and screamed at each other. Quite often the argument was over money.

On one particular night, I remember my mother throwing expensive Wedgwood china at my father and hearing it shatter into many tiny fragments. My mother loved that china. In breaking it she was hurting no one but herself.

One of my patterns became the destruction of anything that I cherished. When I got something that was of value I either lost or broke it. Once I learned where this pattern had emerged from, I could observe the tendency and replace it with something else. With money, it was no different. Any money I got slipped through my hands, always leaving me living paycheck to paycheck.

My money rollercoaster continued because of another pattern which emerged from another childhood event. After my parents divorced, the arguments stopped. My father, who had been frugal, was no longer there to rein in my mother's spending habits. When pay day came my mother would buy me very expensive stuffed animals and other gifts. We would also go out for dinner, something I loved. I associated her paycheck with fun and indulgence.

With this pattern the money inevitably ran out within days and I can remember periods of time with hardly anything in the fridge. It wasn't uncommon to have hot dogs, canned beans and not much else in the house while we waited for my mother to get paid. I have memories of my mother picking up partially smoked cigarettes off the street to smoke them when she was desperate. Once payday came again there would be groceries, toys and a fresh carton of cigarettes.

On one occasion, when I was about five years old, we had very little in the house, and I was hungry. My mother was at work so I took Monopoly money to the store to try and buy food. I remember the shock and embarrassment when the clerk laughed. She had no idea that we had nothing at home.

As an adult, my money pattern was to purchase things that made me feel good. Often these were items that I couldn't afford. I would buy designer sunglasses, beautiful clothing, handbags and jewelry in an effort to feel wealthy. I would then live on very little for the following two weeks until the next paycheck. I was repeating the cycle even though I had resented how my mother raised me; I was living into the same pattern.

By the age of nine, when I went to live with my father, it was different. I received an allowance, which I had to earn, and my father gave of his time as opposed to buying me things. This served to teach me how to value money differently and my paradigm began to shift.

My father ran our family restaurant business with his mother. They worked exceptionally hard. My dad and my grandmother were focused on production, day and night. This reinforced my work ethic and also my belief that if you want to make money you have to work hard.

In high school I desperately wanted to fit in. I envied the girls who had two parents at home. Divorce, in our small town, was an ugly word and children were very much ostracized if their parents were not together. I lived with my father, which only made the situation worse.

Because we owned a business, people thought we were wealthy. I wanted to fit in and thought that if I had the right clothes it would make up for my lack of the "right" family. I worked at three jobs to make money over the summer. In the day, I worked in a tea room as a server. In the afternoon I would go to another restaurant and bus tables. On other days I worked at a sports store.

I was so busy all summer that I saved my money. At the end of the summer my dad took me shopping, where I spent every dollar that I had saved. I bought the latest and greatest brand-name clothes. I was so excited to wear them in the fall. I had a great wardrobe and no money. This was a pattern I would not break until two decades later.

My spending habits did not change as a young adult. Much like my mother, I spent money as soon as I got it. But fortunately, like both of my parents, I was a hard worker. Basically I would work multiple jobs, earn the money and then spend it. It always felt like a long time between paychecks.

Even as an entrepreneur, I have always maintained multiple streams of income. At some level I didn't trust myself to survive on a business owner's income. I always kept a steady job on the side. When I started my personal training business, I managed part-time at a fitness club and taught aerobics at another. When I bought my health club I taught nutrition at a college. The harder I worked, the more money I made. The more money I made, the more of it slipped through my hands.

It would take bankruptcy, losing a business, becoming homeless, attending business seminars and reading over a hundred books on financial literacy to break my patterns. Today, my relationship with money is entirely different. When money comes in a percentage is saved, bills are paid and then discretionary items may be purchased. It took a long time to get to this place and my objective for you, in this chapter, is to fast track you with some of the advice I have learned along the way.

You may be in great shape financially or you may be struggling. You may have an exceptional degree of financial knowledge or you may not have much at all. You may have your own income or you may be reliant upon a partner. As women, regardless of where we are at financially, there is always room to grow. Once our fundamental needs are met, we are able to contribute at the level we desire and there is money to cover emergencies, education and life's adventures – we are in a great place to *have it all.*

An Affair to Remember

"Every man I meet wants to protect me. I can't figure out what from."

— Mae West, *Entertainer*

From outward appearances Mary had it all. She was beautiful, fit, had two kids in a posh private school, lived in a perfectly appointed, exceptionally landscaped home, drove the newest model of Mercedes, lunched at all the right places, attended the hottest benefits dressed in designer couture and was on the arm of Peter, her financier husband. Mary was the envy of many of her friends.

One day, while looking for Peter's passport for an upcoming family trip, Mary found a letter tucked in his desk. It was from a woman, to Peter, expressing her love, talking about their last sexual encounter and how she couldn't wait to see him again. Mary felt as though someone had punched her in the stomach. She couldn't believe that Peter was having an affair. Like any woman—or man—who has been the victim of adultery, she saw her well-appointed life as a well-appointed lie.

I met Mary at a women's retreat I was running. She had quietly kept to herself until Sunday when we covered the topic of money. As I espoused the importance for women to have one hundred percent disclosure of finances with their partners, Mary's hand shot up and she asked to share her story.

After she confronted Peter, he denied the affair. Mary waved the conspicuous letter in his face and he claimed that the woman was a lunatic. There had been no affair. Mary wanted to believe Peter so she backed off, but in her heart she knew he had been unfaithful; there had been other signs that in retrospect she could now see. She hired a lawyer.

Peter asked Mary to give him three weeks to make things right. He suggested they book a romantic getaway and talk things through. He gave her gifts. He was on his best behavior.

In the meantime, Mary's lawyer demanded the couple's financial statements. Mary had given Peter control of the accounts and she truly had no idea how much money they had. She knew they were well off and that bills were always paid. There had been luxury vacations, no question of Mary's trips to the spa or purchases of new clothes for her or the children. She had a vague idea of their situation; however, truthfully, she didn't know how many accounts there were, if there were savings or how much money Peter made.

Mary decided to postpone the divorce after the weekend away; however, she did make a decision to pursue financial transparency with Peter. The lawyer came back and revealed that although there was money, the assets amounted to approximately $300,000. Mary had recalled one bank statement with a seven-figure balance, but she hadn't paid much attention to it. All of the banking was in Peter's name and it almost always went to his office.

What Mary later found out was that during the three-week forgiveness phase that Peter had asked for, he had moved the majority of his assets off shore. Because Mary had always allowed Peter to control things she was powerless. If she left, she would get half of their assets; however, she would have to prove that there had been more, find the trail and spend a long time in court fighting for her share.

Because all of the accounts were in Peter's name, Mary only had access to a bank card that she used for groceries, and a credit card for purchases for herself, the kids and the home. Peter had threatened to block her access from these accounts; Mary didn't even have a joint bank account, so if he did this and she left, she wouldn't have any money whatsoever until the lawyer was able to hash out an agreement, and that could take months or years. Mary was trapped.

When Mary was done telling us her story, there were many open mouths. She told all of the women in the room that above all else, they should never give away their financial power. Women needed to see every bank statement, have their names on accounts, have separate accounts, be party to financial decisions, and ideally have full disclosure with their partners.

From my own experience, of once burying my head in the sand financially and giving away my power in a relationship, I will say, "never again." As women, regardless of whether we are the income providers or not, if we are in a marriage, we need to have full financial transparency. Of course, when we get married, we believe it is going to last forever, that our partner will be faithful and that nothing "bad" will happen. Unfortunately statistics tend to differ, with approximately fifty percent of all first-time marriages, over sixty percent of second-time marriages, and eighty percent of third-time marriages ending in divorce.

As we go through this chapter, I encourage you to keep an open mind. You may be doing some of these suggested things already and you may find other tasks hard. No matter what, do not be like me or Mary and give away your power. I am not a trained financial professional; however, I have transcended financial hardship, learned a great deal along the way and know that in life, we will have times of challenge and having access to money is going to assist us with these moments.

Your Life By Design—How Much Will It Cost?

"There are people who have money and people who are rich."

— Coco Chanel, *Designer*

Consider, for a moment, your ideal life. Where would you live? What would your home look like? What kind of car would you be driving? Where would you vacation? What would your family be doing? What would you be contributing to and how much? What would you be doing with your time? The average woman struggles with these questions because she has shrunk her dreams; reality has become a poisonous pill, swallowed to ensure that a woman doesn't dare ask for anything in her life that she doesn't deserve.

The truth is that you can *have it all*; we all can. We can create our lives by design. We can live in the home we desire, travel to the places we wish, and essentially spend our days doing what we please. It may feel like a long way from where you are now to where you dream of being; however, nothing is impossible. We can have what we want and the first step is to imagine it. People can take away a lot of things from us, but dreaming and our imagination are things that no one can touch unless we let them.

Designing your life, initially in your mind, is something that every woman is doing either deliberately or subconsciously. With websites like Pinterest, where we can pin our favorite dresses, homes and vacations, to the ever-popular magazine industry, where we pour over designer homes and clothes, women are constantly imagining what life could be like and there is an entire industry devoted to the visual richness of our dreams.

Take a moment right now and contemplate your ideal life. List all of the annual expenses that would go into supporting that life, from your mortgage, car payment, groceries, contribution, travel, education, savings and anything else. Next, add an additional fifty percent for taxes. Once you have this number, you now have a target. That target may feel like a long way away; however, anything is possible once we know what we want and have the faith that it will show up in our lives.

You may choose to create a vision board to have images that support your dream. Take a sheet of presentation board and paste on it the images of the life you want to create. Put this where you can see it at least once per day. Vision boards are powerful tools to enhance our ability to make manifest the life we want to create. I have been using vision boards since 2004 and so much of what I have put on these boards has come true.

It is never too late or too early to start dreaming. Regardless of your age, know that you can design your life. Start right now.

Getting in the Financial Driver's Seat

"A good goal is like a strenuous exercise—it makes you stretch."

— Mary Kay Ash, *Entrepreneur*

Now that you have a clearer picture of where you want to be financially, it is time to take a look at how you are going to get there. Some of the topics we are about to cover may be uncomfortable, such as getting life insurance for your children, dealing with wills or reclaiming your financial partnership with your spouse. Money is not always an easy subject to begin with, and delving deeper into areas such as death, make it tougher still.

One thing that you can be assured of is that getting through this work will be rewarding and give you greater power. As women we always want to have our pulse on our money and additionally we deserve to have a say in how the finances of the household are run. Although many women, over eighty percent actually make the primary decisions for household expenditures, we still under-earn men by over twenty percent and in some cases much more depending on the type of job

When it comes to money, and the issues surrounding our money, it is imperative that we co-share the driver's seat if we are in a partnership, or be at the helm if we are single. Many women I know have fallen victim to near devastation due to poor financial decisions. From one friend who lost almost ninety percent of her savings due to an incompetent financial advisor, to another friend who lost her child close to the time her husband was laid off, many women have been ill prepared and uninformed about their money.

To put ourselves in our financial driver's seat, we will be using the following lessons:

1. All Things Have an R.O.I.
2. Read books and attend courses on financial literacy.
3. Interview successful people.
4. Use prosperity conscious language.
5. The Laws of Money.
6. Have multiple streams of income.
7. Open multiple bank accounts.
8. Find a financial advisor with a proven track record.
9. Plan for those "life happens" moments.
10. Adopt a *Have It All* attitude.

Lesson One—All Things Have an R.O.I.

One of the greatest lessons we can ever learn is to understand R.O.I. (Return On Investment). Everything has an R.O.I. My dad taught me at an early age to "not do anything unless it makes you money." He was referring to business and financial decisions, although we can expand this to any purchase we make. Ultimately, there are things we do which do not make us money. All things, however, have an R.O.I.

Let me explain. If you go to the bookstore and buy a romance novel you will not likely make much money from reading it. However, if you read the book, relax and are more productive in your career or business, and your performance increases, you may get a positive R.O.I.

If you go to the bookstore and buy a book like the one you are reading now, and apply the principles and become more productive, get healthier, have more fulfilling relationships and claim your financial power, you are definitely receiving a greater return on your investment.

Let me share with you a real-life example:

Two of our great Step Into Your Power students, Marcy and Tom Blackwell, listened to a goal-setting CD that I had created, every night for two months. During this time the income from their business went from $3,000/month to $6,000/month. Let's take a look at the R.O.I.

Original investment:	$29.99 for the CD set
Net increase in income:	$3,000.00
R.O.I.	10,000%/month

That is a great R.O.I. Additionally, Marcy and Tom own a business so they can write off the CD. This increases the value of the investment.

Everything you buy, every book you read, every audio you listen to, and every course you take has an R.O.I. Women often purchase things looking for immediate gratification. We think nothing about buying a new handbag because we like it; however, what we are not thinking is about the R.O.I. We may also not be considering how much money we had to actually earn to buy that same handbag.

Let's take a look at the following example:

Cost of the handbag	$200
Before-tax income required to earn to purchase the handbag	$400

You see, before we even begin to enjoy that bag we must understand the number of hours we had to work to buy it and ask ourselves if it truly has a positive R.O.I. in our lives. The next time you consider purchasing something that is non-deductible, remember that it is not just the ticket price, it is the before-tax income you had to earn to be able to purchase the bag that matters.

In the business world, it is fully understood that all investments have an R.O.I. When interest rates are low, then long-term investments like T-Bills and G.I.C.'s actually will yield such a low R.O.I. that they do not even keep up with inflation, actually decreasing the original value of the money.

Your home may or may not have a positive R.O.I. I had friends who lost their home in the financial crash of 2008-09. Part of it was due to poor financial planning and part of it was the perception that the home would increase in value. In the past, a home was considered an asset; however, depending on the market you live in, you may be better off treating it like a liability.

What homeowners tend not to consider is that just because the home increases in value, it does not necessarily give a positive R.O.I. By the time we pay property taxes, maintenance, H.O.A. or condo fees (if you have them), do upgrades, and landscaping, we may walk away with what we perceive as a profit after a sale; however, we failed to look at how much money we spent living in that home. The only R.O.I. you should expect from your house is an emotional one.

The same is true of cars, which depreciate the moment they leave the lot. In fact, most items we purchase, unless we have a business, are liabilities. I have long advocated that women have a business in order to take advantage of legitimate tax deductions on things that normally would yield a negative R.O.I., such as your mobile device, computer, internet service and other items, as governments favor business owners to fuel the economy.

Take a moment to contemplate where your money goes. Do you have investments that are yielding a positive R.O.I.? Are you spending money without considering how much you have to make to purchase an item? Are you able to take legitimate tax deductions? Are you looking at purchases from an R.O.I. standpoint? Start today in growing your R.O.I. awareness on anything you direct your money to.

Lesson Two—Increase Your Financial Literacy

The most successful women have a good pulse on financial literacy. They read or listen to books on money, they take courses and they are plugged into the world of finance. This has been a powerful tool in turning my financial situation around; I became an avid devourer of financial literature.

Financial books and courses can yield a positive R.O.I. in many ways and additionally can be a tax write-off if you have a business.

Increasing your financial literacy will change your life. The greatest financial minds have shared their secrets with the world. A good book or course is the outpouring of thought from a brilliant mind. Some of my favorite financial books are listed below. I have read a few of them more than once.

- Rich Dad, Poor Dad, by Robert Kiyosaki
- The Richest Man in Babylon, by George C. Clason
- Think and Grow Rich, by Napoleon Hill
- Why We Want You to Be Rich, by Robert Kiyosaki and Donald Trump
- Secrets of the Millionaire Mind, by T. Harv Eker
- Rich Woman, by Kim Kiyosaki
- Retire Young, Retire Rich, by Robert Kiyosaki
- Think Like a Billionaire, by Donald Trump
- The Bible
- The Alchemist, by Paulo Coelho
- Psychologically Unemployable, by Jeffrey Combs

My library is constantly growing and our children are also keen readers. One of the greatest gifts you can give a child is the love of reading. Books are important and CD's and courses are equally so. When you have the opportunity to connect with someone who has "been there and done that," the experience can be life-changing.

Commit to becoming a lifelong student of finance. Grow your understanding of money and how it works. Train your mind to think like the millionaires and billionaires of the world. Ultimately, it is said that we become much like the people we spend the most time with; thus by reading books by prosperous people, we shift our thoughts to prosperity consciousness and our lives, in turn, begin to change.

Lesson Three—Interview Successful Peopley

The sad truth is that the majority of people get their financial advice from those who are broke as opposed to those who have become successful. My decision to interview successful people was critical to my success and I found that many people were willing to share their challenges as well as their strategies for creating wealth in their lives.

Whether you want to advance your career, change your career or establish yourself in the world of business, it is imperative to learn from those who have done it before. Their wisdom, learned over time, can fast-track you to getting to where you want to be.

Something to consider is that any woman can change her circumstances. She can become a self-made millionaire or billionaire. She can excel in her field. She can create a life by design. Today, many women are paving the way in industries and fields previously dominated by men. From technology to the board room, there are more and more women holding high-profile, high-powered positions.

Find a woman who has achieved something you want to create in your life. You can find successful women in your local region at Chamber of Commerce events, women's networking events, specialty workshops and even online. Ask a successful woman for a few minutes of her time. Find out how she became successful, what challenges she faced along the way, what books she read, how she structures her day and what she might have done differently.

Here are a few sample questions to use when interviewing:

1. Why did you choose your current occupation/business?
2. Who were your mentors?
3. What are your favorite books?
4. Have you ever had setbacks, and if so, what did you learn?
5. What are your daily habits?
6. Are there any seminars you recommend?

7. What are your goals?
8. How long did it take you to become successful?
9. Do you ever get frustrated? If so, what do you do?
10. Do you make an annual business plan?
11. What advice would you give someone in my position?
12. What are your greatest strengths?

Lesson Number Four—Use Prosperity Conscious Language

In interviewing successful people you will begin to notice that they choose words that have greater prosperity consciousness. Instead of saying, "I can't afford that," they are more likely to say, "I am finding a way to acquire it." People who are successful understand that words are indeed powerful and that whatever is spoken is very likely to come true.

I know a woman who is constantly lamenting her lack of money. She lives paycheck to paycheck, barely getting by. Everything in her life is a crisis and the more she talks about how she can't afford things, the more bills she receives in the mail.

One of the easiest things we can do to shift to financial freedom is to use language that empowers us. Over the years, the people who I have met who are the most broke have also been the most negative. The wealthiest people I know tend to be the most positive. The wealthiest women I know do not think in terms of not being able to afford or do something. When given a choice, the *have it all woman* chooses "both."

When I had reached rock bottom my language was extremely negative. I agonized that I couldn't afford things. I thought constantly about debt. I worried about how long it would be until payday and on and on and on. We often hear that our outer world reflects our inner world. I am here to share that our outer world is exactly what we are painting on the canvas of our minds. The thoughts we think are being manifested right before our eyes.

If we focus on debt we get more. If we focus on wealth we get more. If we focus on health we are healthy and if we focus on disease prevention we become diseased. What we think about comes about in vivid reality.

In learning to monitor my language, I realized that my words were the simplest thing to change. It didn't cost me anything to start choosing different language and the rewards were seemingly immediate. When we change our thoughts, the outer world must catch up and match exactly what we are focusing on in our mind.

Make the decision to shift your language now. The faster you embrace the language of the wealthy, the faster you will attract new opportunities to your reality. One of my favorite expressions is, "If you think it's easy, it's easy; if you think it's hard, it's hard. Either way you are right." Using affirming language is one of the most powerful steps in creating wealth.

A quote dating back to over 400 B.C. says, "Words are the physicians of a diseased mind." For thousands of years it has been understood that words are powerful. Words are the paint on the canvas of our mind. The question for you is, what have you been painting?

Let's take a look at some common negative language around money, and some positive replacements.

- I can't afford that vs. I am in the process of attracting the money to buy that.
- I am broke vs. I am becoming cash-positive.
- I am in debt vs. I am in the process of building my assets.
- Investments are only for the rich vs. I can invest any time I choose.
- I am never going to get ahead vs. I will move forward.
- There is no opportunity for me vs. There are opportunities everywhere.

You can change your mindset by asking some simple questions. When the dark side of your mind comes forward telling you what is not possible, remember to shut that down and focus only on the simple truth that whatever you want in this life is out there right now. The more you focus on having it, the faster it is attracted to you.

Lesson Number Five—Understand the Simple Laws of Money

Law # 1—Pay Yourself First

Until I understood the simple laws of money, I stayed in the pattern of living paycheck to paycheck. There was never enough money left at the end of the month. I had no savings, and my debt was unmanageable. The creditors were calling and I got sick.

At the time, I was embarrassed. How could I have let myself get into such a terrible financial state? I didn't understand my patterns and I had never been taught the simple laws of money. The truth was that the majority of my income was coming from one source. Previously, before the downturn, I always had multiple streams of income, but at the lowest point I was living on income from my business which was operating at a loss!

When I became an entrepreneur many people said, "Susan, pay yourself first." These were some of the most successful people I knew, and yet I didn't have the courage to ask them what that truly meant. I had heard the number ten percent often; however, I couldn't truly imagine having ten percent to save.

It was at a Jim Rohn seminar that I fully grasped the concept. Mr. Rohn was speaking on the simple laws of money. He said that they dated back to the Bible and that the wealthiest people he knew subscribed to these teachings. It was in that room and in that moment that I clearly understood that principle. Just three years later I was a millionaire and that was my proof that the principles work.

The principle of paying yourself first means that when you receive a paycheck or any kind of income, you take ten percent of the after-tax income and allocate it to savings. You will never touch the principal and it is never too late to start. That ten percent goes into a savings account, 401K, RRSP or whatever investment account you have. The interest and the principal grow and it is always there for you. This ten percent should have a low degree of risk so that a volatile stock market does not wipe it out.

I see a lot of women who get seduced into investments and when a tragedy such as 9/11 occurs, their entire savings is eliminated. Educate yourself and keep this ten percent in something conservative. Find an investment vehicle that yields a strong percentage above inflation and yet has the least degree of risk. You will be thankful.

What If I Am Upside-Down In Debt?

If you have a great deal of debt you must still pay yourself first. Regardless of debt, we age, have illness, have tragedy and all sorts of other lifetime events. It is more expensive not to pay yourself first, believe me, I have learned from experience.

I too, was once heavily in debt. I thought that I couldn't pay myself first. I was so wrong. When I started to pay myself first and set aside this ten percent, my income continued to grow. Start today, regardless of the situation you are in. It may be small – just a few dollars every week – however, one thousand dollars is made up of one thousand dollar bills, and one hundred thousand is made up of one hundred thousand dollar bills. The bottom line is to start now and do it with every source of income you have.

Law # 2—Tithe or Give

The Bible also urges us to give ten percent. This means that for every paycheck you receive, you should give ten percent away. You may be thinking that you can't do this one either. However, to fully grasp this you must understand the law of reciprocity. It simply means that when you give you receive.

I was working with a woman who was a professional network marketer. Ella was in a place where her income was stuck, and she was blocked in all other areas of her life. Her health was poor, her finances were a mess, people were not returning her phone calls and her leaders were not producing. Every time we got on the phone she complained about her life. It was all about Ella.

One day I asked her which part of her life included contribution. She was silent as she looked into all of the dark corners of her existence. She thought she was truly contributing in every area of her life, but her giving came with expectation. If she worked with one of her people, she expected them to produce. If she helped a stranger she expected something in return. Even with her own health, it was all about buying time. Ella would even indulge in ice cream one day and plan to work out the next – but tomorrow never came.

I suggested that Ella start making her life about something more than herself. I encouraged her to sponsor a child through World Vision. The sponsor amount was only about $40/month and that covered vaccinations, clean water, food and education. I have personally been to a World Vision development program locations and know firsthand the work that goes into assisting one child. $40/month is a bargain.

Ella and I went on the website together. She chose the first child to pop up on her screen, a boy from Thailand. Ella pulled out her credit card and took the plunge. She was fearful. Ella had never really committed to anything in her life. The first thing to happen was that Ella felt joy. She then cried because of the impact. She showed her family and friends her newly sponsored child. She felt incredibly peaceful.

The best thing happened a few weeks later. Ella's income doubled and she became a six-figure earner. Ella had learned the fundamental law of reciprocity. When you give, you eventually receive, but only if you expect nothing in return.

You may be thinking, I am in debt – I can't afford to give anything. That is not true. I hear a lot of people say that they will start contributing when they become rich. They never become rich. Start now.

You may start with something like sponsoring a child or contributing to your church, synagogue or mosque. The donation may seem like very little to you. However, if you can give and expect nothing in return, the abundance will eventually flow.

Charitable donations are usually tax-deductible up to a certain percentage. Consult your accountant or national government website to see which percentage applies to you. Not all charities are registered, so if you intend to utilize a tax receipt, make sure the charity is indeed registered nationally.

Find a charity or church that resonates with you spiritually. My husband and I donate to numerous causes, but our criteria for donating is that the charity must be improving the lives of women and children. Chris and I have funded two schools in Africa, supported a trauma centre in Cambodia, and also sponsored, at the time of writing this book, 20 children through World Vision. We also support charities in North America.

Winston Churchill said, "We earn a living by what we do. We make a life by what we give." Ask yourself, how do you want to be viewed in one year? Two years? Three years? At the end of your life? My grandmother was a great philanthropist. She gave to many causes that were in her heart. Even though she has since passed, she is still known as a great lady in her community.

You do not have to give a lot of money to make an impact.

Donate your unused clothes to a women's shelter. Buy baby food for your local Food Bank. There are so many things you can do to make a massive impact. Begin today.

Law # 3—Become Cash-Positive

The term "cash-positive" simply means that your total assets are greater than your liabilities. You can never truly be financially free until this happens. Of course, the bottom line on the cash-positive quotient is simply a reflection of your net worth.

In grade ten, I took a business class and we were taught how to make a balance sheet. On the left hand side we listed our liabilities, which in grade ten were not many. On the right hand side we listed our assets, which were also not many. After subtracting our liabilities from our assets we were either cash-positive or cash-negative.

Becoming cash-positive is imperative for long term goals, and unfortunately, many women do not know if they are cash-positive or not. I once had a client who lamented about how much debt she had. Once we looked at all of her finances and did the C.P.Q. (cash-positive quotient) exercise at the end of this chapter, she actually realized that she was $50,000 cash-positive and not as mired down in debt as she thought.

Knowing your C.P.Q. will help you gauge what your next steps should be. Perhaps there are liabilities you can get rid of. Perhaps there are assets you can sell to pay off debts. Maybe you can downsize in order to become cash-positive. Fundamentally, I feel this is something we should be teaching in classrooms. If children fully understood the importance of always being cash-positive, they would most likely grow into more responsible adults and we wouldn't have many of the financial tsunamis we have today.

A final word on the C.P.Q. is that I invite you to do this with your partner. Having transparency with money is an important step to maintaining a healthy partnership. I also suggest that if your children are ten or older that you also share what is going on in the family finances. Children are extremely intuitive and if there is any tension about money, they will more than likely pick up on it.

Law # 4 – Understand Credit and Pay Down Bad Debt

There are only two types of credit – good credit and bad credit. Good credit is money borrowed at a percentage which is lower than the return on investment of the asset we are purchasing. For example, if we borrow money at 5% and purchase a rental unit and are able to net a 15% gain then we have made a smart decision about using credit.

Conversely, bad credit is where we use borrowed money to purchase things which have a negative R.O.I., like the handbag mentioned earlier in this chapter. When we borrow money to buy items that we cannot afford and pay a premium of interest on a balance, usually around 18%, we are creating bad credit.

Credit cards are one of the most seductive credit vehicles on the planet. The average person has three or more credit cards and is lured to sign up for new store credit cards because of the promise of additional discounts or enrollment gifts. Sadly, multiple credit cards are a surefire way to become out of control with debt and I highly advise against it. On a personal note, I have only two credit cards. One is for personal use and the other for business.

Whatever credit card you use, make sure you accumulate something in return. For Chris and I, we use a card which gives us airline miles. We can then take fabulous trips that we could not write off for tax purposes. For personal expenses I use a credit card which I must pay off monthly – an American Express. I love the Amex card because you cannot carry a balance. If you are a big spender with a small paycheck, I encourage you to use a card that you must pay off. It creates a greater awareness of debt responsibility.

Take a minimum of 10% of your income and use it to pay down debt. If your debt is out of control seek out a debt counselor and work with your bank to see if you can consolidate your debt. Do not bury your head in the sand. Many credit card companies and collection agencies are open to working with you if you can create a repayment strategy.

Law # 5—Invest In Education

Ongoing education—whether it is your financial literacy, a degree or diploma to increase your job prospects or learning a new skill to create a backup plan—is something that wealthy people choose to do. You may decide to take five to ten percent and invest in seminars, books, courses and programs designed for personal growth or developing new skill sets. Investing in yourself is the greatest investment you can make. The more you grow, the more ability you develop to create change.

Take a look at what you can afford to do. Even if you are on a strict budget, get a library card and start working on yourself today. You do not have to spend a great deal of money to advance yourself, but you will have to invest the time. A statistic a wealthy friend shared with me is that the average person will spend almost 3 years in their car driving. If you listened to audios from the greatest financial, personal empowerment and business minds you would get the equivalent of a university degree simply by driving in your car.

As women, we are great multi-taskers. We can listen to audios while we work out. We can read empowering books instead of numbing ourselves with television. We can attend personal development seminars with our girlfriends. We can watch TED Talks online. There are endless possibilities when it comes to our personal education.

Law # 6—Create a Budget and Live on the Remainder

If you save ten percent, tithe ten percent, use at least ten percent to release debt, reinvest five percent into your education, you will be left with fifty-five to sixty-five percent to live on. There are great APP's available for budgets and other online resources. Ask anyone you know who works in the financial world for their recommendations.

This money is divided among your day-to-day expenses, such as mortgage or rent, groceries, transportation, phone, computer, etc. If you own a home-based business, then you will be able to write off some of these expenses and that deduction can be exceptional at tax time. If you are living within your budget and following the simple money rules and not incurring new debt, eventually you will be cash-positive and in a place of true financial freedom.

Lesson Six—Have Multiple Streams of Income

Since I was a teen, I have always had multiple streams of income. In high school I worked at three jobs so I could make extra money for college. In the day I worked at a tea room, in the afternoon I sold clothing, and in the evening I bused tables at a restaurant. Three part-time paychecks earned me a full-time income over the summers.

When I went to university, I taught fitness classes and pre-school camps. This provided me with multiple streams of income, although it was employee income. After university, I worked for the government and the schedule was often midnights, so the only other thing I could do to make extra income was teach fitness.

My dad always said that as long as you have skills you will be fine. He encouraged me to become a certified fitness instructor, personal trainer, nutritional consultant and much more. He also taught me how to drive a stick shift, because he explained that "both tractors and race cars require manual transmission."

When I owned my health club I also worked as a personal trainer on the side and taught at a local college. To this day, I love checks. They are sublime. I no longer teach fitness or do personal training. However, I do have multiple streams of income from multiple businesses, investments and contracts.

The road to financial stability and truly understanding how useful multiple streams of income were, came with many lessons. When I lost my health club I still had my skills, and was able to walk into a management position with what was then the world's largest health club chain. As always, I did personal training and nutritional counseling on the side. I thought I was being smart by having all of these other sources of income, but I did become exhausted and got quite ill.

It was thanks to a great mentor that I first read Rich Dad, Poor Dad, by Robert

Kiyosaki. I was absolutely stunned by the simplicity of the message. I was already a business owner, but the majority of my income was from the "employee" quadrant. That meant that someone else was dictating how much money I was worth. Additionally, none of it was passive income, which meant that I had to work for every penny of it. If I didn't work, I didn't get paid.

Many professionals are in this boat. Chiropractors, lawyers, accountants, physicians, therapists and many others only get paid when they work with a patient or client. If they are in a partnership they will get paid when they do not work. But it takes years to build a reputation as a professional, and the price to buy into a partnership is often so high that it takes years to pay it off. To become a professional requires years and years of education and is often accompanied by student loans in the hundreds of thousands of dollars.

There are passive streams of income that have work on the front end and residual income on the back end. People who write or record hit songs, authors, investors and many others receive royalties, dividends and income. They could be on vacation, or sleeping when it happens. The likelihood of my performing a chart-topping song wasn't very great because I lacked interest in it. To write a best-selling book required experience in the area I wanted to write about. My investment ability was contingent on initial capital and so that left only a few options. Fortunately, I found one of the best.

Thanks to Robert Kiyosaki, I also became passionate about network marketing. I attempted several companies until I struck gold and became a millionaire with one of them. Network marketing is one of the best business models in the world. It allows the business owner a small start-up compared to a franchise or organically growing a business, and people learn more about themselves here than any other place.

Network marketing also encourages personal empowerment. The most positive, open people I know are also network marketers. The industry has also received some bad press but with investors such as Warren Buffet, and accolades from Donald Trump, T. Harv Eker and others, the network marketing industry is reporting record growth. It also creates more millionaires, to my knowledge, than any other industry in the world.

There are many good network marketing companies out there. With most you can get started with an investment of under $2,000. Compare this to a franchise or starting your own business, and the investment is indeed quite small. To be classified as legitimate, a product must exchange hands. Make sure that your initial startup fee includes more than a training manual.

For women, network marketing has provided another stream of income since the late nineteenth century. My book, Inspired to Win in MLM, discusses the features to look for in a solid network marketing company.

There are many ways to create multiple streams of income. You can start a savings account with even $20.00/month and at the end of the year you can put that money into a larger investment; the interest is another stream of income.

You can get a certificate for a new skill such as bookkeeping or personal training. You can do this part-time, and make a significant amount of additional income. While this income may not be passive, it will assist you to become cash-positive and build additional multiple income streams, including a portfolio.

Portfolio income is just one of the possible streams. As I mentioned before, you may elect to do a network marketing business or run a small business from your home. If you are an executive with little time, ask your financial advisor about other potential streams such as rental income and other investments. When you have multiple streams of income you are not relying on just one source.

Financial storms will continue to erupt; these things go in cycles. Those who are best prepared for financial challenges are those who do not rely on one singular source of income. Take stock right now and look at how many sources of income you currently have. Ask yourself if one of the sources no longer provided income, would you be able to survive on the remainder and for how long?

As women, we should never rely solely on one singular form of income. Having learned this in the past, it is not a lesson I would choose to repeat. A great mantra for this segment is this – multiple forms weather multiple storms. Make a conscious decision right now to have at least three multiple streams of income flowing in within the next two to five years.

Lesson Seven—Open Multiple Bank Accounts

With the arrival of internet banking it has never been easier, or more affordable, to open multiple bank accounts. Personally, I have more than five. You may want to start with just two or three. In order to get your financial head on straight, it is key that you know where your money is going and what it is allocated to. Good financial institutions will let you have multiple bank accounts for free if only one is a checking account.

The first account is your primary one. This is where the day-to-day expenses come from. You may have a check draft account or debit account.

The second account is savings. This is where your ten percent goes. It may stay in cash, although that would not be as prudent with such low interest on most savings accounts. Ideally you will leave some in cash and the rest you will invest. It is a good idea to set up a regular contribution to a 401K, or RRSP if you are Canadian. This way money is automatically deducted from your account and goes straight into your investment account.

The next account may be allocated for debt payment. Take ten percent and put it into this account every time you get paid. At the end of the month you can make your debt payments from this money.

If you wish to do a fourth account you can put your tithing money here. At the end of the month you can make your donation and feel really good about what you are supporting. I donate online using my credit card so I simply move money from my tithing account to my credit card after I make the donation.

I also have a "kid's account" into which I put money every week. This money goes towards their education in addition to their education savings plans. As I am self-employed, I also have a "tax account" where I allocate money weekly towards my income tax.

The most important strategy around these multiple accounts is to use them effectively. As soon as any income comes in, allocate it to the appropriate account. Having multiple accounts has helped many women become more organized financially and is a wonderful way to truly get a grasp on where your money is going.

Lesson Eight—Find a Financial Advisor with a Proven Track Record

Even after my financial reversals, when I was making $15,000/year, I had a $250,000/year attitude. I knew that I would be a six-figure earner again. I was in a position that was temporary and although I didn't know how it was going to change I knew it was going to change.

The first thing I did was establish some multiple streams of income. I started in network marketing again. I saw nutrition clients on the side and was able to get to an income of $40,000/year within a short period of time. I wasn't at $250,000 yet but I was closing the gap.

I met an investment advisor at a women's networking event. She also believed that I would increase my income. An interview with a previous investment advisor hadn't been so positive; the woman had actually laughed when I told her that I would be multiplying my income sixfold.

Working with my investment advisor was refreshing. We communicated often and met, in person, twice each year to do a review.

Another friend, an investment advisor, offered to do a portfolio review and I found out I was paying an exorbitant amount in fees. My portfolio was heavily invested in mutual funds, which have the highest management fees, and I could be doing much better. Although I had a great relationship with my advisor, I decided to move my portfolio because ultimately my objective was to have my money working for me and not be working harder to pay more fees.

Every one of us deserves to partner with an advisor who believes in us and has our best interests at heart. Ask successful people for referrals of investment professionals and financial planners. If you are an entrepreneur, work with an advisor who works with other self-employed people. If you are single you may want to partner with someone who specializes in single-family incomes.

If your current financial advisor isn't serving you, do not hesitate to find someone new. This is your money and your future. Your advisor is essentially your business partner, so find someone you trust and get to work. Every wealthy person has a team, and your advisor is a big part of that.

Before you go see an advisor, figure out your annual income, your current debt, your retirement goal date and how much you intend to live on. Your advisor can then assist you in creating a strategy that works.

Lesson Nine—Plan for Those "Life Happens" Moments

During our lifetimes it is very likely that we will face "life happens" moments, including the death of a family member, personal injury or illness, property damage, and so forth. These events are emotionally and financially draining. Unfortunately, many women are ill-prepared for these times, and sadly, the financial stress is often a tipping point to greater distress when things happen.

Preparing for death, ours or a loved one's, is one of the toughest things we can do. No one wants to imagine outliving their child or partner; however, these things happen on a daily basis. I have had friends who have been widowed at a young age or had to deal with the death of their child. Other friends have been faced with the unexpected death of a parent. In many cases there is no financial preparation for the costs associated with long-term illness or a funeral.

Something to consider is purchasing funeral insurance for your immediate family and having discussions with your parents as to whether or not they also have provisions. It is heart-wrenching to think of losing your partner, child or parent; however, if you also have to deal with the expense of the funeral, how much more stress will that add to the situation? Funeral insurance, especially for children, is not very expensive and although it makes me sick to even fathom the passing of a child, I have seen it happen on several occasions and it left the families with a big financial burden in every case.

The next area to look at is your will. A significant percentage of women do not have a will and this leads to confusion and even arguments after death. In the United States, there is an estate tax, which is to be paid out before any heirs receive anything. In other countries there are similar taxes. Regardless of finances, having a will does not ensure that your wishes will be met but it does ensure that your wishes will be known.

If you have young children make a decision as to who will care for them should you pass. Also – will there be enough money to provide in your absence? Do you have life insurance to cover the costs of their education and upkeep? Do you have specific wishes for how they will be raised? Do you have any items that you would like to go to a particular individual? Are there provisions for charity? Who makes the decision to "pull the plug" if you are in a coma?

We do not want to think about our own mortality, let alone that of someone we love; however, this is one of life's moments and taking a proactive approach is always best.

Lastly, aside from death, there will be times of emergency. Chris and I once had our furnace breakdown, beyond repair, and the bill was $6,000! We were only bringing in about $32,000 annually at that time and we had to borrow money from Chris' parents. It was humiliating. We were not prepared for life's emergencies and we were very lucky to have people in our lives who could assist.

Set aside some money every single month for emergencies. The goal should be eventually to have six months' worth of living expenses in a cash account that can be accessed 24/7. The average person does not have an emergency fund and would not last beyond two weeks if they lost their job or had an emergency.

Take responsibility today and get your will done, purchase appropriate insurance and absolutely start your emergency fund right now.

Lesson Ten—Adopt a *Have It All* Attitude

The *Have It All Woman* has a *have it all* attitude when it comes to money. She doesn't say that she "cannot afford something," and she doesn't spend out of her comfort zone. When it comes to savings, becoming cash-positive and leading an abundant life, she wants it all and doesn't hesitate to create a team of people who support her goals.

The *Have It All Woman* has multiple streams of income. This may come in the form of investments, a part-time job, real estate, network marketing or some other source. She does not question "why;" instead she asks the question "how" to find out exactly how to get what she wants.

The *Have It All Woman* does not value herself by what she wears or what she drives, she values her self worth by what she does to make an impact. The *Have It All Woman* is truly free because she is in the process of creating her destiny.

The *Have It All* attitude is about living now. It is about deciding right now that you are the master of your finances and taking responsibility for your life. No one is going to save you, and winning the lottery is very unlikely. You can be your own lottery and move forward.

The evidence is compelling that women all over the world are living rags-to-riches stories and not marrying into them. You can create something from nothing because no matter what happens no one can take away your heart, your skills or your dreams. The *Have It All Woman* knows that she is in charge of her life and the only person who can stop her from getting what she wants is that person in the mirror.

Use the Four-D Principle for Money

Decide to take control of your finances.

Define your ideal life and exactly how much it will cost to create that life.

Delete financial activities that are sabotaging your goals.

Definitive Action: Increase your financial literacy, create/update your will, understand your CPQ, get financial advice, have a financial transparency conversation with your partner if you have one and purchase appropriate insurance.

Have It All Affirmation

Money flows easily and freely to me.
I have all the money I require and more.

- HAVE IT ALL WOMAN EMPOWERMENT EXERCISE -

Knowing Your C.P.Q.

List All of Your Assets and their Estimated Value

- Cash __________
- Securities __________
- Pension Plan __________
- Life Insurance Policy __________
- Estimated Sale Price of Home Less Commissions, etc. __________
- Land __________
- Real Estate Other than Primary Residence __________
- Net Worth of Car __________
- Jewelry __________
- Art __________
- Other __________

Total ______________________

List All of Your Liabilities

- Credit Card Debt __________
- Mortgage __________
- Line of Credit __________
- Misc. Debt __________

Total ______________________

Deduct your Liabilities from your Assets __________________ C.P.Q.

Now that you have your C.P.Q., it is either positive or negative. Wherever you are right now, this is your starting point. The goal is to get you to neutral and then to positive. The wealthiest people in the world owe money. However, it is often business-related, and they maintain a positive C.P.Q.

The ultimate peace is to become one hundred percent cash-positive, and spend only what you have, not what you will be making in the future. Debt is a noose around your neck. It is worth it to look for ways to create more income for yourself, so you can release debt forever, even if it means extra effort in the short term.

CHAPTER EIGHT

Step 8: Giving Back

"Blessed are those who can give without remembering, and take without forgetting."

— Princess Elizabeth, *Asquith Bibesco*

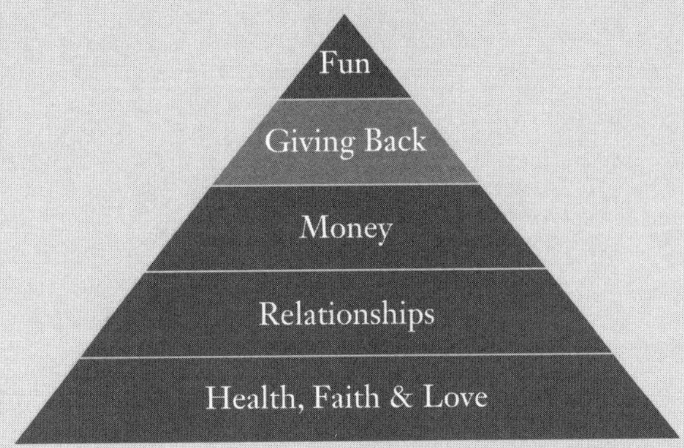

CHAPTER EIGHT

Step 8: Giving Back

Rescuing Babies from Jail

"These children have done nothing wrong. They are simply caught in something they do not understand."

— Pushpa Basnet, *Child Advocate*

Pushpa Basnet had a problem. Well, she didn't exactly have a problem; she was aware of a big issue and couldn't get it out of her mind. Incarcerated Nepalese parents were forced to bring their children to live in the inhuman conditions of Nepalese prisons as an only option. She decided to do something about it; she decided to foster these children until their parents were released.

Through her work and efforts, 140 children have been liberated from jail. She is called "Mamu" by the children, an affectionate name with maternal connotations. In 2012 Pushpa won CNN's Heroes Award and is using the money to liberate more children. Of those rescues she recalls a five-year-old who had been raped by her father. This child was abandoned by her mother, but she was forced to go to jail with the very man she lived in terror of. Babies and older children are also under Ms. Basnet's protection and at the time of her prestigious award she was only twenty-eight.

In a country where poverty is rampant and archaic laws combined with political insurgence make it tough to survive, let alone thrive as a woman, Pushpa Basnet is proof that we can always make a difference regardless of our circumstances.

Decide That You Can Make a Difference

"Walking with a friend in the dark is better than walking alone in the light."

— Helen Keller, *Advocate*

Regardless of what is happening in our lives, we can always make a difference in someone else's. We can give of our time, our resources, our possessions and even our words. We never know when today's simple kindness may be tomorrow's lasting impact.

My dear friend, P.K. Smith, runs a charity called Impact Malawi, which does sustainability work in the country which boarders to the north of South Africa. On one visit, P.K. brought blankets to a remote village as it can get very cold in Malawi at night. Many people live in mud huts without insulation or even a proper roof. On a subsequent visit, many months later, these villagers credited P.K. with saving lives from the simple gift of used blankets. Something so simple had changed lives.

Look around your home and see, even if you have done the clutter clearing from chapter one, if there are things, such as clothes, that you can donate to the local women's shelter. Find out if there is an organization you can volunteer with (although not before reading the next section). If you have the resources, explore options for where your money could best be utilized. Silently wish everyone well, even strangers that you pass on the street; even this act of contribution can make a difference.

You are an amazing woman. You can impact the lives of others. Begin today by simply deciding that you can change a life and that even if your contribution appears small, it can have a massive impact.

What Is Important To You?

"Carry out a random act of kindness, with no expectation of reward, safe in the knowledge that one day someone might do the same for you."

— Diana, *Princess of Wales*

When I walked into the trauma center in Cambodia my heart leapt out of my chest. There was a four-year-old girl holding a teddy bear. I asked one of the staff why she was there and he said two terrible words: "raped repeatedly." I knew in that moment I would work for these girls and for the years to follow, I worked with World Vision, the organization overseeing the trauma center where girls who have been sold into brothels, raped and assaulted, had come to find shelter, medical and psychological counseling, therapy, education and the community of other girls who have experienced similar trauma and atrocities.

Having money makes it easier to give, though I started giving when I didn't have a lot. After reading numerous financial and spiritual books I understood that tithing was important. I made a decision to donate what I could until ten percent became a realistic number. My first contribution started with a small monthly donation to Amnesty International, an organization that fights for people who have been the victims of human rights abuses. Next I began to give to the food bank, the Salvation Army and other organizations working with women and children.

I also gave to my church. We built a school in Africa. We have contributed to the UNHCR, the United Nations High Commission on Refugees, and many others. Essentially, Chris and I are passionate to help women and children around the world.

Chris and I sponsor twenty children through World Vision. At only about $40 a month per child, this brings us joy. We love getting letters and progress reports. We also love sending letters. When I was in Cambodia I visited two area development projects and I witnessed firsthand how sponsorship dollars work and it left a lasting, positive impact on how I choose to give.

We have all of their photos hung up in a room just off the kitchen in our home. If I am feeling a little sad or tired I look at those faces and become instantly inspired. How can I afford one down day if I can save a life?

Giving has also provided us with an awesome opportunity to travel. Yes, we love a good luxury hotel now and again, though going into the field and hearing stories where we know we can make a difference is truly life-changing.

In the years of running the *Have It All Women's* Weekend, we partnered with

Sistering, the largest women's drop-in center in the downtown core of Toronto. We raised money for writing projects, capital expenses and programs. We learned, through our partnership, that there isn't a lot of distance between the average woman and a life on the streets.

As women, there will be no end of people and organizations vying for our time and wallet. The most important thing to remember is that we do not have to say "yes" to everyone. In fact, it is much better to make a decision about how you would like to direct your giving and direct your efforts in that direction.

I have girlfriends who are passionate about causes such as autism, cancer, eating disorders, animals, orphans, and more. Ultimately they are driven by what fuels their soul. When we are able to give from a place that mutually fulfills us in some way then the giving becomes effortless. If our giving is done out of a sense of obligation then it will be draining. Decide what is important to you and let go of anything that is not in alignment with your vision.

I also suggest that you create a philanthropic mission statement. Ours is very simple – "We lovingly contribute to projects that uplift the lives of women and children around the globe." In having a mission statement for our giving it also creates parameters for what we do not choose to give to. The more successful you become, the more people will ask for your money and time. When you have a clearly defined mission statement it is easier to make a decision of whether to support a cause or not and this will remove any overwhelm or resentment in your giving.

Giving Gratitude

"Be thankful for what you have; you'll end up having more. If you concentrate on what you don't have, you will never, ever have enough."

— Oprah Winfrey, *Television Personaity*

I once asked one of my mentors the secret to her success. She was a multi-millionaire, cancer survivor and a real *Have It All Woman*. She told me that every day she wrote at least ten things she was grateful for. She said that when she started to list the gratitude items daily, her life became extraordinary. I embraced this process and it changed my life too.

As we begin to truly stand in a place of gratitude for even the smallest things in our lives, our view of the world shifts. This shift in perspective changes how we interact with the world, now coming from a place of deeper appreciation; the world in turn, shifts how it responds to us. It is as though we were living in black and white and are suddenly seeing color for the first time.

Initially it may be challenging to find ten items every day and I suggest beginning with the simplest of things such as clean water to drink, air to breathe, a roof over your head, the sound of a child's laughter, the kindness of a stranger and so forth. Whatever the case, being grateful for what you have leads to more abundance and fulfillment in all areas. The exercise will begin to get easier and easier.

As we make a conscious decision to express and give our gratitude to the world, we will indeed begin to receive appreciation in all forms, flowing freely back to us. Openly give your gratitude. If someone does something for you, thank them with a full heart. If your child, friend or family member does something wonderful, let them know. The essence of having it all is knowing that in many ways we already have it. Expressing our gratitude for the life we have is the launch pad for greater and greater levels of abundance to come.

Use the Four-D Principle for Giving Back

Decide that you can make a difference.

Define what causes are important to you.

Delete anything that you are giving to that does not feel right.

Definitive Action: create a giving statement, find a way to contribute that is in alignment with your goals, contribute time and/or money to something that brings you joy and give from a full heart.

Have It All Affirmation

My contributions make a difference.

- *HAVE IT ALL WOMAN* EMPOWERMENT EXERCISE -

Create a Philanthropic Mission Statement

Decide what causes, groups and organizations are important to you. Write a one to three-line mission statement describing what you are contributing to and you will contribute to it. Use this mission statement to create clarity and focus around your giving.

CHAPTER NINE

Step 9: Girls Just Want to Have Fun

"I've realized that being happy is a choice. You never want to rub anybody the wrong way or not be fun to be around, but you have to be happy. When I get logical and I don't trust my instincts—that's when I get in trouble."

— Angelina Jolie, *Actress and Humanitarian*

CHAPTER NINE

Step 9: Girls Just Want to Have Fun

Fun—What Fun?

"You only live once, but if you do it right, once is enough."

— Mae West, *Entertainer*

Sandra lay quietly on the sofa. How long had she been there? Days? Months? Years? She seemed to recall seeing her daughter earlier in the day. Thank the Lord that girl was self-sufficient; Sandra had been directing Kylie's life from that sofa for a long, long time.

The illness had stricken her body so much that there had been layers upon layers of medication. There were drugs to numb the pain, drugs to deal with the nausea caused by the pain drugs, and drugs to help with the anxiety caused by feeling so hopeless. This was no way to live.

Sandra had once been vivacious, confident, energetic and an athlete. She had thankfully been really good with her money too, so when she was diagnosed with the illness she didn't have to go on assistance. She wasn't sure how long the money would last but she was sure that she couldn't go on living on this damn sofa any longer.

Sandra made a decision. She was going to turn this around. She was going to change her life. She was going to start living again. Enough was enough. She started with her diet, making a decision to detoxify her body. As she started to feel better she began to exercise again. Slowly but surely, she started to feel human.

She was angry that she had wasted so many years and she felt that she had a lot of time to make up for. This is when she made a decision to things that brought her joy; she was going to have fun as if her life depended on it.

Instead of going to her daughter's hockey games she was going to work with the team because that would be more fun. Instead of sitting at home feeling sorry for herself she got out there and started dating because that was much more fun than spending Friday night alone. Sandra started laughing again. She started feeling happy again. Today, Sandra has come a long way from that sofa. Sandra and I have known one another for a long time and it brings me such joy to see her laugh and smile again.

Sadly, there are many women running their lives from the sofa; I used to be one. Smart, strong capable women who have fallen down so many times that they lack the energy to get back up. They have lost their joy and thus their will to continue on. Life has become so serious that many women can't remember the last time they had a really good belly laugh, which is tragic as laughter is truly such good medicine.

In creating our *have it all* life, we want to bring fun into every aspect of our life pyramid; we want to smile more, laugh more and experience joy in our day-to-day existence. Fun is at the top of the pyramid because it should permeate through our entire lives. As women we have so much going on, we are so busy with the doing that we forget about the being. Having fun is one of the simplest ways to bring joy, harmony and greater fulfillment to our lives and the focus of this chapter is to help you do just that.

Dance Like There Is No One Watching

"Ever notice how 'What the hell' is always the right answer?"

— Marilyn Monroe, *Actress*

One evening I attended a party at an exclusive Scottsdale resort. At the gathering were business executives and their spouses. One of the guests surprised the host by flying in a band from New Orleans. As the music started pumping, people moved cautiously in their seats. A friend's wife was bopping away beside me so I grabbed her and we got up to dance. Within minutes most of the room was up dancing too. It took this other woman and I to get things started but soon enough there were plenty of people having a lot of fun.

Much of life has gotten quite serious and we look to YouTube and other social media outlets for things to find funny while we sit in front of our computers and mobile devices. It is as though much of the world has lost the ability to let loose and have fun. One of the key reasons is that people are generally very self-conscious. This isn't something we are born with; children tend to be very open in their expressiveness, creativity and play.

As adults we concern ourselves more with how other people think. Sadly, for women especially, the less we laugh and have fun, the more cortisol we create. Cortisol, a stress hormone mentioned previously in Chapter Three, will cause us to gain weight, have sleep disruptions and many other things. By choosing to laugh more, play more and have more fun we actually can lower our stress levels and become much healthier.

You can choose to have more fun. Put on music and dance while you do the dishes. Go to a stand-up comedy club. Watch funny movies. Get your girlfriends together for a "no seriousness allowed" evening. The most important thing is that you learn to let go of what other people think. This is your life and it is much too short to be taking it, or yourself, too seriously.

What Do You Do For Fun?

"Children reinvent your world for you." — Susan Sarandon, *Actress*

Fun is perhaps a lost art in the twenty-first century. Somehow we have become so serious that stress and disease are at an all-time record high. Laughter is such wonderful medicine that there are stories of people recovering from horrible diseases because they choose to focus not on the disease, but on laughing and having fun.

When we laugh, smile, and play it releases endorphins. It creates a natural high. No wonder children play all the time. They are addicted. As we grow up and have to work, pay bills and deal with the challenges of adulthood, we lose our sense of playfulness. Losing that part of yourself, or perhaps never discovering it, can lead to a life lacking in fulfillment. The time is now to start having fun.

What do you do for fun? Do you like to hang with the girls? Do you like to ski, take a class, watch a movie, go for a pedicure, check out the museum, read a trashy novel, have a bubble bath while perusing a gossip magazine, or get romantic with your partner? What does having fun mean to you? Could you do more of it? If so, what would your life look like?

Make a list of all of the fun things you like, and would like to do. Divide the list into three sections – those things that are free, those things that you could afford to do weekly and those things which you would save for. Next schedule in something fun every week; give yourself something to look forward to. Another great thing to do is delegate time to someone else every week and let them choose a fun activity. Children, especially, love this.

The Fun of Re-Inventing Yourself

"I'm undaunted in my quest to amuse myself by constantly changing my hair."

— Hillary Clinton, *Former Secretary of State*

My friend, and hairdresser, once counseled me never to get my hair cut when I was angry, hormonal, going through a major life change or postpartum. His wisdom was right on the money, but despite his words I found myself cutting off ten inches of hair on my thirty-fifth birthday and spent the next two years growing it out. I wanted something new and different. Naturally, I regretted it the day after, although for one day, with my new slick bob, I felt like a different person.

My reinventions have been many over the years and gone beyond hair. I have been lean, curvy, long haired, red haired, highlighted, dressed all in black, dressed in color, soft spoken, "kick-ass" and everything else under the sun. Every reinvention is an evolution of myself. Next on my list is to hire a stylist. That will be fun.

As women we can get into a rut. We keep the same makeup, clothing, hair, friends, interests and habits for years. Have you ever seen one of those television shows where they make someone over and it totally changes them? Often the person resists the change, if only for the cameras, and then voila – just like Cinderella, she is transformed.

Reinventions can be subtle. You may change your hair, your makeup, how you dress, your outlook, your interests and even your dreams. Reinventions can also be more significant, such as getting married, having a child, getting divorced or moving. The truth is that every major junction in our lives provides us with the opportunity to step out as new incarnations of our former selves.

Oprah Winfrey is a prime example of a woman who constantly reinvents herself. Oprah stays true to her heart while changing her hairstyle, look and her interests. Oprah does not waver from her belief in justice and equality. That is what allows her to be a chameleon while maintaining her integrity.

Reinventing yourself is fun and I highly recommend it. Whether you change your hair, your nails, update your wardrobe, learn a new language, take a cooking class, become a vegan or whatever else you choose to do, a reinvention is a wonderful way to create a fresh start in your life or celebrate a milestone. I encourage you to check out websites such as Instyle.com and others, where you can upload a photo of yourself and view how you would look with different hairstyles and clothing. Even exploring the process of a reinvention is fun in and of itself.

Lastly, I encourage you to start having more fun. Get your joy back. Be adventurous. Let loose and laugh more. You never know what tomorrow will bring but you do know for sure that you have today. Time is precious and to experience our lives through the lens of joy is one of the greatest gifts we can give to ourselves and others.

Use the Four-D Principle for Having Fun

Decide to bring fun into more areas of your life.

Define fun activities you can do.

Delegate time to fun every single week.

Definitive Action: book time with friends and family members and let them choose fun activities to do. Schedule time every week to do something fun.

Have It All Affirmation

My life is full of laughter, ease, joy and fun.

- *HAVE IT ALL WOMAN* EMPOWERMENT EXERCISE -

Create Your Fun List

Make a list of at least one hundred things you can do for fun. Divide the list into three distinct segments—those things you can do for free, those things that you can do weekly but may have a cost and those things that you would save money for. Schedule in time for something fun every single week.

CONCLUSION

Let's celebrate! You have made it to this point. My prayer and wish for you is that you have made some significant changes in your life and are on the journey to having it all. Like any journey, I have no doubt that there will be some bumps in the road, but do not let that deter you. By choosing to live into the life pyramid you prepare yourself for life's journey. By setting a solid foundation you fortify your life against the more challenging times.

Becoming a *have it all woman* isn't necessarily a destination which we arrive at and maintain; it is an ongoing work in progress. There will be moments where we do not feel balanced or lack the conviction to take the next step and thus I encourage you to lean on your life pyramid; staying dedicated to the principles outlined in this book.

I want to acknowledge you for your courage, strength and heart. I invite you to create a *have it all* life and be an inspiration for women everywhere. You are Divinely created. You are capable beyond measure and you can truly be, do and have anything you dream.

With Love and Appreciation,

Susan

PERSONAL ENDORSEMENTS

"The *Have It All Woman* is a must read for anyone looking to be empowered. All women have the ability to be a force and to create a legacy. Susan Sly shows them how."

— **Dr. Tony O'Donnell**, Bestselling Author, Speaker, Radio/ Television Personality

"Susan Sly is an incredible entrepreneur with a passion for assisting women."

— **John Gray**, NY Times Bestselling Author of *Men are From Mars Women are From Venus*™

"Susan Sly flat rocks! She is one of the most caring, cool women I know in the business world. If you have any chance to get in front of her or work with her, do it! Your check will love you for it!"

— **Todd Falcone**, Network Marketing Mastery

"Susan Sly is a magnificent woman who literally pours greatness into other people in such a way that they feel it and want to live into that greatness. I have had the opportunity to work closely with Susan on many projects and see first-hand how she uses her brilliance, creativity, vision, clarity, and heart-based consciousness to assist others to be their best. Susan inspires by example and living her own life with integrity and intention. I am honoured to call Susan Sly my friend and mentor!"

— **Camille Lawson**, Nutrition, Hormones, Sexuality, & Wealth Consultant

"Susan is a wonderful example for women of all walks of life that they can *have it all.* What Susan teaches is applicable in the real world. A proven model that not only inspires and empowers women and families, but more importantly ensures results."

— **David Wood**, Author and Speaker

"Susan is one of the smartest people I have come across and truly knows what it takes to become healthy today and stay healthy for a lifetime."

— **Brandon Steiner**, Chief Executive Officer of Steiner Sports Memorabilia, Inc.

"Susan Sly is an exceptional entrepreneur and leader. Susan's teachings, specifically her 'Shift' meditation series, address the real problems that many sales professionals encounter when they begin their journey into free enterprise. I highly recommend visiting Susan Sly's website, reading her blogs, and downloading The Shift Meditation series."

— **Tom Bukacek**, Co-Author of Bestseller *Marketing Miracles* with Dan Kennedy

"Susan Sly is the real deal. She walks the talk. There isn't a single word she says that she doesn't live. I have benefited greatly from knowing and learning from her. I've invited her to teach my clients how to be more effective and they rave about the results they achieve with her training. She gets my highest recommendation!"

— **Matthew Ferry**, Author of *Creating Sales Velocity and Ridiculous Bliss*

"Susan Sly is a mentor that every woman deserves in her life. She is a lighthouse for women guiding them to purpose, inner strength, and success. She has a mind of excellence and a heart of service. Susan has taught me, by example, how to be a better woman and believe anything is indeed possible. She is an absolute gift to this world and your life will be better for just knowing her—I know mine is."

— **Dottie Lessard Brownsberger**, Author, athlete, triple organ transplant survivor